# Palms Up!

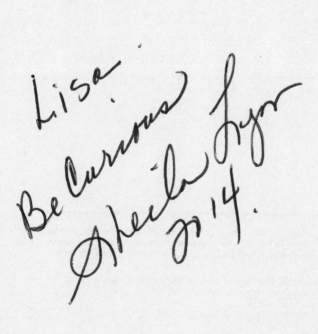

Lisa.

Be Curious Lynn

Sheila Lynn

2014.

# Palms Up!

## A Handy Guide to 21st-Century Palmistry

### Sheila Lyon

& 

### Mark Sherman

Berkley Books, New York

**THE BERKLEY PUBLISHING GROUP**
**Published by the Penguin Group**
**Penguin Group (USA) Inc.**
**375 Hudson Street, New York, New York 10014, USA**
Penguin Group (Canada), 10 Alcorn Avenue, Toronto, Ontario M4V 3B2, Canada
(a division of Pearson Penguin Canada Inc.)
Penguin Books Ltd., 80 Strand, London WC2R 0RL, England
Penguin Group Ireland, 25 St. Stephen's Green, Dublin 2, Ireland (a division of Penguin Books Ltd.)
Penguin Group (Australia), 250 Camberwell Road, Camberwell, Victoria 3124, Australia
(a division of Pearson Australia Group Pty. Ltd.)
Penguin Books India Pvt. Ltd., 11 Community Centre, Panchsheel Park, New Delhi—110 017, India
Penguin Group (NZ), Cnr. Airborne and Rosedale Roads, Albany, Auckland 1310, New Zealand
(a division of Pearson New Zealand Ltd.)
Penguin Books (South Africa) (Pty.) Ltd., 24 Sturdee Avenue, Rosebank, Johannesburg 2196,
South Africa

Penguin Books Ltd., Registered Offices: 80 Strand, London WC2R 0RL, England

This book is an original publication of The Berkley Publishing Group.

PRINTING HISTORY
Berkley trade paperback edition / July 2005

Library of Congress Cataloging-in-Publication Data

Lyon, Sheila.
    Palms up! : a handy guide to 21st-century palmistry / Sheila Lyon & Mark Sherman.
        p. cm.
    ISBN 0-425-20266-6
    1. Palmistry. I. Sherman, Mark. II. Title.

BF921.L96 2005
133.6—dc22

                                                                        2005043621

PRINTED IN THE UNITED STATES OF AMERICA

10  9  8  7  6  5  4  3  2  1

Sheila and Mark dedicate this book
to their parents—who instilled in them
a boundless curiosity about life
and its workings.

## ACKNOWLEDGMENTS

We would like to thank the hundreds and hundreds of people who allowed us to use their stories (and their hands) in *Palms Up!* Without their time and generosity, there is little hope that we could have created a book like this, a look at palmistry that brings it out of the Middle Ages, through the New Age, and into the twenty-first century.

# CONTENTS

*Introduction*    The Future Is Now: Palmistry in the
Twenty-First Century                                    *1*

1 . How Long Are Your Fingers?                          *9*

2   The Mighty Thumb                                    *29*

3   The Rest of the Digits                              *61*

4   The Palm                                            *109*

5   What the Mounts Say About You                       *179*

6   The Four Hand Styles                                *203*

7   Fingerprints                                        *233*

8   Sheila's Hand Games                          263

9   Squares, Triangles, Stars, and
    Other Markings                               309

10  A Few Last Words                             335

# Introduction

## The Future Is Now: Palmistry in the Twenty-First Century

Palmistry is not really about fortune-telling; it is a method of character analysis, and our aim in this book is to make it accessible. Our take on palmistry encourages readers to use palm reading as a way to develop new and intuitive ways for thinking about personalities and prospects—and as a strategy for getting out of the rut of habitual thinking. Palm reading is not, *definitely* not, about being taken into the dark interior of a Gypsy's tent where a woman wearing hoop earrings and a bandanna will mutter darkly about your future. In the here and now, palm reading offers a way of reinforcing your intuitive thinking; it gives you a new way to explore your life and attitudes, your potentials and possibilities. Palm reading is also about social exploration, about the most fascinating feature of our universe, more fascinating than the distant stars or the subatomic regions—the human realm, ourselves and others.

This is the territory of palm reading, where we explore the mystery of human personality. Why is one person drawn to people, whereas another is the very model of introspection? Why are some of our friends interested in facts, but others are on a perpetual search for the Loch Ness monster? Palm reading can help you create your own personal map of the qualities you will need to find in another if he or she is to be a good romantic fit for your life and lifestyle. Do you want to determine if a particular candidate for Mr. or Ms. Right is The One you've been searching for? Palm reading offers shortcuts to guide you in your search. And palm reading can give you both a clear idea of the kinds of jobs you're best suited for and the tools for making yourself shine during the interview. *Hint:* A glance at your interviewer's hand can provide clues to the best communication style to adopt for presenting yourself as a likely job candidate.

Palm reading is fun. We have seen palmistry enliven parties that were thought dead on arrival. Palm reading allows people to get close to one another and share their personal worlds in a positive way. Curiosity seems built into the human DNA; and, no matter how skeptical you are, you're always curious about anything that can give you insight into the way those closest to you think and behave—not to mention something that can give you more insight into yourself!

As active palm readers ourselves, we're interested in getting *you* out among your friends and loved ones, using this ancient art in a way that's fun and upbeat. You'll find palm reading a fascinating journey: part performance art, part a way of exercising your deepest intuition. Once you've stood among a group of friends, pointing out the features of their hands and sharing what palmistry has to say about their thumbs, index fingers, Life Lines, and Heart Lines, you will be the life of any gathering.

And you'll never look at hands the same way again.

*Palms Up!* will introduce you to palm reading in *our* world, a world radically different from when palm reading was practiced and written about by Vedic-speaking monks, German medieval occultists, and Romany girls in Gypsy caravans. The palm reading we will teach you is practiced in a world of cell phones, e-commerce, and casual travel among the continents. It's no longer a world where people marry once, have a score of children, work at a single occupation, and shuffle off this mortal coil sometime in their middle to late thirties. *Palms Up!* reflects the fact that we read palms in a world where our readers' experience likely includes practicing monogamy until they get it right; having two, or three, or more occupations; and, perhaps, toward the end of the twenty-first century, deciding just how indefinitely long they *want* to live.

This book takes a look at some of the myths of palmistry—with an eye toward dispelling them—while exploring some contemporary twists on old truths. For example, in *Palms Up!* palm reading, a short Life Line *does not* mean a short life. We have done charity work in assisted-living facilities and have read the palms of ninety-year-old men and women with Life Lines no more than two inches long! Multiple marriage and children lines no longer mean multiple spouses or children; we look to these lines to understand the *interaction* in relationships.

After reading this book, you'll be able to use the lines on the palm to explore life's everyday situations. You'll be able to tell whether the person you've just met is too timid to take *any* risks or if he's comfortable jumping right into a situation and surfing the changes as he goes. You'll also know whether that certain someone you're interested in can leap into decision making or if she prefers to plan a course of action over the long term. With a little practice, *Palms Up!* palm reading will enable you to identify a friend's, a loved one's, or a perfect stranger's basic approach to life. Is he a my-way-or-the-highway personality? Or is he willing to share the steering wheel of life? You'll be able to look at a person's baby finger and tell whether she's more likely to be a daredevil or a master of caution. At a party you'll amaze people by being able to determine which of the partygoers is most likely to have a Harley-Davidson parked in the garage. At a job interview, you'll be able to size up the interviewer and give yourself an advantage in the interviewing process. At a bar you can use *Palms Up!* palm reading to tell whether a person is interested in playing the field or more likely to be passionately looking for one special person.

*Palms Up!* will surprise you. It focuses on using palmistry as a contemporary strategy for exploring one's own personality—for fun, with the emphasis on entertainment. You'll be able to use this book as a strategy for helping free yourself from the habitual mental ruts people can get into. As you master the techniques of *Palms Up!* palmistry you'll begin to make discoveries about yourself and about your closest circle of friends. Why is it that you feel so special about the true friends you've found in life? What is it that makes them special? You'll find the answers in their palms.

# Right or Left: Which Hand Should I Read?

Before we get started, we should talk about which hand to read when you begin reading palms—right or left? You should look for the dominant hand of the person whose palm you're reading. Dominant hand? The dominant hand is the one you use to write with, to sign your checks, to turn the pages of this book. The overwhelming majority of human beings, by some quirk of genetics, are right-handed. So, in most cases, you'll be reading the right hands of the people whose palms you read. But if a person is left-handed, that is the palm whose lines you will look closely at.

Why?

For modern palm readers, the dominant hand is the active hand, the hand that speaks of those attributes you are busy using (actively, naturally) in your life at the present time. Your other hand, the nondominant or passive one, speaks about potential, those qualities you possess that are part of your personality and talents but are not being specifically called on at present.

It boils down to a simple rule: If a person is right-handed, read his right hand. If he is left-handed, then read his left.

What if someone is ambidextrous? Our recommendation? Let her choose. Her intuition (the heart of palm reading) is bound to steer her straight.

# How Long Are Your Fingers?

The length of fingers is a major clue to personality.

Hold your hand, palm side up, in front of your face. Keep your hand completely open, but relaxed. Look at the relationship of the fingers to the palm of the hand and compare the length of the palm and the length of the fingers. Is your palm longer than your fingers? If so, you have "short" fingers. If your fingers are longer than your palm, you're long fingered. If your fingers and your palm are equal in length—a rare occurrence—you have what we call a well-balanced hand.

If you're going to master the art of *Palms Up!*

palm reading, there is no better place to start than with finger length. The simple fact of how long a person's fingers are will give you valuable information about who he is, and, even more important, how he views life and the people he encounters. Whether he's long or short fingered, you'll be able to know in a heartbeat whether he's deeply into details or whether he prefers an eagle's-eye view of the world around him.

Knowing this can give you an instant advantage. With just a single glance you can quickly give yourself valuable clues to interacting with other people—whether in an important job interview or at your favorite bar. In this chapter, you'll develop techniques that will allow you to speak *their* language and make your points more engagingly.

# Long Fingers

## Deeply into Details

Long fingers on a hand indicate someone who is deeply into details. This is the kind of person who, usually from very early in life, learns to handle and love the intricacies of the world that we live in. These people very often find themselves drawn toward positions in life where they deal with details and schedules. We refer to people with long fingers as *Sherlocks*. Like the literary figure Sherlock Holmes, they both see and observe the world, minds alive and on the lookout for the details that fascinate them. Alice is a perfect example of the long-fingered Sherlock sort. She has long, finely architectured fingers, much longer than the average. She is a stunning dresser and spends hours getting a look that is "just right." She is a fanatic networker and the possessor of a truly heroic address book, with connections that would be the envy of any politician. Alice is an event planner, and a quite successful one. Details are Alice's stock-in-trade; she loves them. Long-fingered people have excellent focusing skills. They want to achieve certain very specific goals. They want to be able to do whatever they do intensely and perfectly—they want to play Mandelbrot's third concerto in G-minor the way that Nigel Kennedy does. Long-fingered people sign up for French classes to learn to speak French so that, when they go to Paris three years from now in the spring, they will be able to order palais de deux at the Maintenant restaurant near the Rue de Tambours. Are you getting the flavor of this finger trait?

Because of their love of detail, long-fingered people make fanatical collectors. Whether it's philately (stamp collecting), numismatics (coin collecting), or Barbie collecting, Sherlocks are naturally drawn to the command of detail that serious collecting requires. They excel in making quick, skillful verbal comparisons and evaluations among things. If they are into language and writing, they can make good lawyers. If they're into math, they can make good engineers and mathematicians. Those with a more physical bent enjoy any work that involves keeping track of inventory. Another thing about the long-fingered person?

Though they are detail oriented, they are not necessarily organized.

---

### *Palms Up!* Prescription

One of the dangers facing the long-fingered folks is losing their perspective; they may find it easy to get lost in those details and miss the big picture. It's easy for Sherlocks to focus on the minutiae and lose the goal. They can combat this tendency by involving themselves in activities that force them to step back from the details they love so much and to de-stress.

---

## In Relationships

People with long fingers see their relationships in terms of specifics. Again, it is all in the details. If you want a long-fingered partner to remember, think about, and value the moments you've spent together, talk about specific instances. This kind of memory gets her attention.

How do you attract a long-fingered person? If you meet someone out in the world with long fingers who seems like just your type—and you want to be *certain* he notices you—make sure you talk to him in specific terms about who you are and what you want out of life. If he asks you questions, make your answers specific. If a long-fingered person asks you if you've done any traveling, telling her that you spent the summer in Barcelona is not enough. Instead say that you walked Barceloneta beach at five in the morning as the sun was just coming up on the third day of your trip. The wide blue Mediterranean was sweeping away into the distance. The entire city was either asleep or just coming home from the night's festivities. Tell her the way the morning air felt. *This* kind of memory gets the attention of those with long fingers. They collect memories: their own and the memories of those they're attracted to. So if you want to attract a long-fingered person *be vivid!*

On the other hand, if details bore you, you may want to steer clear of a relationship with a detail-oriented, long-fingered type. It's important to recognize and acknowledge this at the outset. Do you want—do you *need*—a relationship with a person who will not be fully happy unless he can express and share his worldview, which seems to include a hunger for the details of everything that occurs in his life? Such a relationship might challenge you to make in-depth excursions into the specifics of whatever interests *him*. Any interest he takes up—whether hobby, vocation, or volunteerism—will be pursued to a depth of detail that can at times be astonishing. Sometimes it can be tricky.

Take Kelli, for example. Her long-fingered partner, Brendan, is deeply into salsa dancing and was eager for her to join the fun. At first, to Kelli, it seemed all about fun and nights with a group of people who loved to dance. As things progressed, however, Kelli was taken beyond her comfort zone. What started as dancing and socializing progressed into a depth of detail and commitment to salsa that was out of her league. She found that she didn't really care whether a particular dance step was Cuban or Columbian. After a night of dancing, long sessions critiquing the dance steps of other couples and the authenticity of the music became tedious for Kelli. What had started as an enjoyable hobby got drowned in details.

The good news is that Kelli and Brendan worked it out. Brendan is still pursuing his love of details. But Kelli no longer goes to Brendan's Cuban percussion classes. They've made the adjustment. Their relationship thrives. But it *is* helpful to know, before embarking on a relationship, where it may lead before you get into those uncharted areas.

In reading the palms of the long fingered, you can appear almost psychic if you make a statement such as this: "You're famous among your friends for knowing things, little details, about the world that no one else seems to know. Am I right?" Because long-fingered people tend to collect things, you can also add to your psychic reputation by stating: "But there's one area that really excites your interest, isn't there? In fact, you've got a collection, don't you?"

As a *Palms Up!* palm reader, please remember to respect the hand and the life of the person for whom you're reading. You may not be as stuck on details as the long-fingered person whose palm you are reading, but you'll be of more service to her as a palm reader if you can take on her perspective, her way of seeing the world, and make it your own for a moment.

One last thing to remember when reading the hand of a long-fingered person—don't be surprised if he begins bombarding you with questions during the palm reading, asking, seemingly, for more, more, more!

# Short Fingers

## The Big Picture

People with short fingers want the big picture. Although they are not allergic to details, they prefer them in small portions. They are bored by, and largely uninterested in, the kind of detail that long-fingered people crave. A good way to remember this quality is to think of them as *Sky Pilots,* traveling quickly around the world, their lofty vantage point allowing them a large inclusive perspective. They may not always catch all of the details, but short-fingered Sky Pilots are very likely to see the manner in which the parts fit together, sometimes in ways that can seem un-canny, even baffling. They are able to make quick, intuitive assessments about things, people, and places. They often display a knack, a natural talent for intuiting when things are out of place, espe-cially when someone is lying.

Jane is a good example of this. She has all the classic traits of the short-fingered person; she's sharp and quick witted. Part of her job is inter-viewing candidates before passing them on to the final hiring committee of her company. We asked her, "Do you use rational, left-hemisphere criteria when you make your final choice? Does intuition play any part in the process?" She told us that by the time she met candidates in the interviewing process, they'd already distinguished themselves with the human resources people, and their ré-sumés had been judged to be a good fit for the company and the position being filled. She said she often gets an instant sense of who the com-mittee will hire. This impression comes in a flash, like recognizing an old friend in a crowd. She gives herself a 90 percent hit rate. Short-fingered people have this knack. Call it gut instinct, intu-ition, or lightning cognition.

In social settings, like parties, people with short fingers circulate, touching base with everyone. They usually have good memories and can astonish people with what they recall, moments they've shared, things they've done.

Short-fingered people tend to be ambitious. They're generalists and see the big picture—they see it all, and they want it all. Although their long-fingered friends want *this* particular thing here and *that* specific thing there, short-fingered people naturally want what they see on the plate in front of them, and beyond. Short-fingered people tend to be drawn to goals that are larger than life.

They like, or more typically, demand, that things be fast paced. They can be like a jolt of espresso to those around them. They liven up any party, but they are easily bored if the pace becomes anything less than manic. However, if boredom can be a problem for short fingers, it can also be a concealed blessing. These people have endless creativity and, when forced to, can come up with the most inventive and intricate ways of keeping the beast of boredom at bay. "Let me entertain you" should be the short-fingered person's slogan.

*Palms Up!* **Prescription**

Short-fingered people should watch out for impatience. Sky Pilots tend to think and act quickly. Because of this, they can be guilty of making snap decisions, and when they do make decisions based on gut feelings, they can often steam-roll others who make their decisions more slowly.

# In Relationships

In relationships, short fingers are fundamentally interested in what details add up to: the big picture. They are not concerned with specifics, with details, like long-fingered people are. Because of this, you'll find that their sense of control in any situation will be based on a general view of individuals and the way they behave. What does romance mean to a short-fingered person? They're looking for an overall sense of good feelings. In matters of love they have the tendency to be accommodating and to adopt a get-along approach with the world. All things being equal, they will be less critical and less willing to argue about details. They will tend to have a don't-sweat-the-small-stuff attitude.

If you find yourself in a situation where there's a short-fingered person in whom you're interested, you'll fare better when you're talking to him if you look to find things in common. Don't be shy about sharing your vision of life, of what the world might be, what might come about in the future. He *will* respond. Why? Because an overall vision of life is what he cares most deeply about. Short-fingered people are great sharers; if you can share what things mean to you and how those things made you think and feel differently, you'll be well on your way to catching the interest of a short-fingered person.

A long-fingered person will ask you, "What did you do?" A short-fingered person will ask you, "Why did you do it?" And she'll be intrigued by the answer. Then she will tell you what it means to her. When you read the short-fingered person's palm, you can almost see her straining to see the big picture. Focus on telling her about her skills and attitudes and how she might develop them. Don't spend too long on any one thing. Shift focus frequently. Since she's easily bored, anything you can do to intrigue her will be appreciated.

# Searching for Mr. Right the *Palms Up!* Way

Let's say you're out on the town with your pals and walk into a place where you find some interesting candidates for companionship. Here are a few quick tips on how to make your moves that will allow you to steer your pals (and yourself) in interesting directions.

If you're long-fingered and spy an interesting dating candidate who has short fingers, know this: Going out with that short-fingered person will be a whirlwind tour. You'll find yourself viewing the world from a decidedly different viewpoint, not from the deck but from the crow's nest, up where the breeze is blowing and the people on the deck below look small and distant. With your love of detail, this can be a refreshing change, to be plunged into a world that is all about the big picture and the way things feel to you. But since you're more into details than your short-fingered partner, the big picture view of life can, after a while, begin to pale for you. Are you ready for such a change in lifestyle? Would you welcome it? Or would you rather take a pass?

If you have long fingers and are interested in a long-fingered person, know that you may spend the rest of your lives arguing over details, but you may be very pleased to do so! With a long-fingered romantic partner, you won't be stretching yourself to see the world from the other person's perspective—you'll share his perspective. The early thrill of hanging out with another person who, like you, has long fingers will come from the reality of finding yourself being instantly and easily understood. Running with a long-fingered partner can be both cozy and exhilarating. Empathy does that. The problem areas in such a match will most often occur during times when stress comes at the romantic duo from the outside world. Money pressures or the stress of dealing with unreasonable relatives are frequent culprits. In such situations, long-fingered partners tend to reinforce one another's negative takes on a problem, causing stress levels to spike. At these times, couples need to be *very* careful to remember that the details they care so much about can sometimes get in the way of their locating big picture solutions to their problems.

# Can Mixed-Finger Couples Find Happiness?

We have read literally thousands of palms from all over the world, and (you may be relieved to know!) we have read the palms of *many* happily married "mixed" couples (one with very long fingers and the other with very short fingers). One thing we've noticed is that these couples are able to adapt to the viewpoint of the person they are in a relationship with. Not to excess; yet they are able to put themselves in the position of their oppositely fingered partner and see the world the way he or she does. So if you're reading palms for couples (or would-be couples!) and they ask, "We have different length fingers, are we compatible?" you can say the unequivocal answer is yes!

Older books on palmistry take a fairly judgmental approach to human differences. Sometimes their take is simplistic: "Long-fingered and short-fingered people can't get along!" As a *Palms Up!* reader, you'll often find yourself changing people's thinking about what different hand characteristics mean. Although older takes on palmistry tend to act as if people with widely different hand characteristics had little hope of maintaining long-term relationships, modern palm readers know—from real-world experience—that this is just not the case.

In fact, we say *vive la différence!*

# Using Palm Reading to Land Your Dream Job

Going to an interview for a job you're supremely interested in landing? Notice the length of your interviewer's fingers and use your knowledge of palm reading to improve your chances of nailing the interview.

If a short-fingered person is interviewing you, make sure that you give him lots of big picture talk. Let him know you have energy and people skills and, most of all, that you are supremely adaptable and able to fit yourself into situations that change quickly. The short-fingered interviewer is likely to be less interested in your specific job experiences and more interested in the skills you possess and how you would fit in with the organization. Remember, too, that interviewing job candidates can become tedious (especially if you're the tenth candidate he's interviewed!); if you sense that you're losing his attention, break the monotony and ask *him* a question. Your ability to shift the focus will give him a break that he'll appreciate. In a relaxed and gracious way, be as interested in him as he is in you. If you focus on showing your adaptability and flexible nature, you'll do well in an interview with a short fingered person.

What if you notice that the interviewer has long fingers? Adjust your strategy! Know she wants to hear about your history and what you've done before this potential job, in a chronological way, one thing after the other. She wants details, details, details. Give her what she wants, and you may just get her to give you the job.

# The Mighty Thumb

The thumb is one of the true superstars of palmistry; it speaks volumes to the palm reader who's willing to listen. In New Delhi, present-day Indian palmists will spend an entire reading exploring just the mysteries of the thumb! There's that much to tell. The thumb is a very special digit—a defining human feature. The thumb is about worldview, the way we look at and approach life.

The first thing to observe when contemplating the mighty thumb is how (and where) it's attached to the hand. How high or low is the thumb set on the hand? A thumb that is set high on the hand will reach up to (or almost to) the first knuckle of the index finger, the tip of a low-set thumb ends right where the index finger begins, at the bottom of the bottom phalange

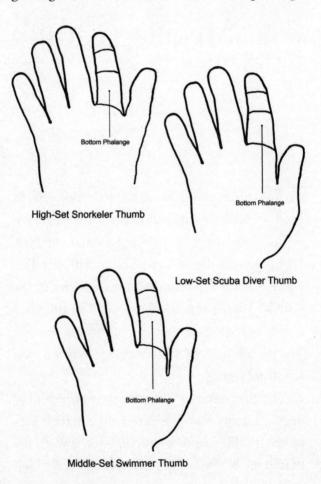

**High-Set Snorkeler Thumb**

**Low-Set Scuba Diver Thumb**

**Middle-Set Swimmer Thumb**

(pronounced, FAY'-LANJ) of the index finger where it meets the palm. A third position for the thumb is to have the tip end somewhere in the middle of the bottom phalange of the index finger. We're going to take an in-depth look at each of these thumb personalities. To get the most out of this chapter, we recommend you identify your own (or a special someone's) thumb style.

# A High-Set Thumb

If your thumb comes far up on the side of the index finger, almost to the top of the bottom phalange, *mobility* and *coverage* are your watchwords. "Just do it" is your motto. We call these thumbs *Snorkelers*. Snorkelers are happiest with a pace of life that's fairly brisk, even frantic at times. Snorkelers have a love affair with mobility; they'll rack up the frequent-flyer miles wanting to see (and do) as much in life as they can possibly manage. They usually make great companions, because they are never static and are enthusiastic, group-oriented people. They have lots of intensity, but it's usually about big picture things. They

tend to take a global approach to their own problems and the problems of the world, and they
tend to look for group solutions to both kinds of
problems. Snorkelers know that life is what you
make it.

---

### *Palms Up!* Prescription

If you have a Snorkeler as a lover or friend, be
prepared to match his or her mobility, because
you'll sometimes find yourself on a thrill
ride hither and yon.

---

When we spot a Snorkeler thumb, we'll look
on the opposite side of the hand (called the percussive side) at the side of the palm just below the
little finger. The fine lines along the percussive
side of the palm are the travel lines. We think of
these lines as the *Kerouac lines* because the person
who possesses a lot of them is likely to find herself
on the road many times in her life. A twenty-first-
century palm reader will interpret the Kerouac
lines like this: The deep lines are the travel you
*must* do, the travel that occurs when you have little

choice. The fine lines are volitional travel, the travel that occurs because you *want* to do it. This differs in a major way from the manner in which travel lines were read in the past, when generations could be born, grow up, enter old age, and shuffle off this mortal coil within eyesight of the homestead on which they came into this world. Travel opportunities (and frequent-flyer miles) had to wait until the late twentieth century to become a common factor in life, let alone palm reading. We frequently see people with very deep travel lines. If you'd like to come across as psychic, say to (don't ask!) the person with these lines, "You're really racking up the frequent flyer miles, aren't you." Then tell him why you're making the statement. You'll impress him.

We have noticed that people with Snorkeler thumbs tend to have more travel lines than people with other kinds of thumbs. There are exceptions, but Snorkelers consistently have more travel lines, and they tend to view travel in a radically different way from others. For Snorkelers, travel is almost always a necessity, as if somewhere deep in their mental makeup they held a vow to see and do.

# A Low-Set Thumb

If your thumb is set low on your hand, its tip rising up only a little more than the crease of the bottom phalange of your index finger, you are what we call a *Scuba Diver*. Scuba Divers ask the deep questions: What is life? What is human identity? Does the mind transcend the brain? Scuba Divers spend significant portions of their time in pursuit of the deep stuff. They are looking for breakthroughs, and their search is conducted with passion and thoroughness. Scuba Divers are look-

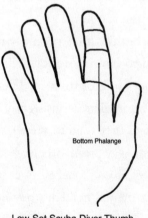

Bottom Phalange

**Low-Set Scuba Diver Thumb**

ing for the ultimate experience or the breakthrough moment, the moment when the whole world seems to open up and shout its secret to the worthy. Scuba Divers require deep exploration to make their lives satisfying. They are prone to misunderstand others, especially Snorkelers.

To Scuba Divers the basic Snorkeler approach to life seems wrongheaded; where's the depth and intensity? If you are a Scuba Diver, you're constitutionally unsatisfied with remaining on the surface of things. This is not to say that Scuba Divers are dark, intense sorts. Scuba Divers are curious about the world (or at least their parts of the world), and they can be a font of unusual details about the way the world works and why it works the way it does. They are often dazzling conversationalists, with an unusual depth of vision that makes them memorable to other people.

Probably more than any other thumb type, Scuba Divers attract followers, people who are captivated and made curious by the intensity and passion displayed by these deep voyagers.

# A Middle-Set Thumb

If your thumb tip stops about halfway between the first knuckle of your index finger and the place where that index finger attaches to your palm, you have a middle-set thumb and are what we like to call a *Swimmer*. In some ways, Swimmers have the best of both worlds. Swimmers get a glimpse of the big picture coverage coveted by Snorkelers, but they are not addicted to variety. This tends to give them a sense of satisfaction with their lives without the restlessness of the Snorkelers' lifestyle and consciousness. Swimmers

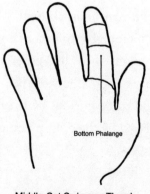

Bottom Phalange

Middle-Set Swimmer Thumb

also experience the intensity and focus that is part and parcel of the Scuba Diver way of being but without losing touch with the more quotidian world. Swimmers tend to have a keen, almost magical sense of perspective and balance. For this reason they often attract people whose lives are in crisis. People seek out Swimmers for their flexibility and sense of connectedness, in short, their rootedness.

Swimmers have definite periods in life when they are attracted (intensely) to the deeps— periods when passion and a quest for intensity get the upper hand in life and take them somewhere rich and strange. But these are only periods. Swimmers are also attracted to going places and thinking global, slipping on the seven-league boots that are the native Snorkeler's footwear to take a look-see for themselves. This sometimes unexpected side of the Swimmer personality gives them an edge that their acquaintances and friends value. Swimmers often fool people, like a book with a bright cover that reveals unsuspected depths or a comedy that, in the end, reveals a serious deep intent that makes it ambitious, a classic.

# Swimmers, Snorkelers, and Scuba Divers

Parties are an excellent place to get the hang of twenty-first-century palmistry. Ask people to show you their palms as if they were directing traffic. When your friends raise their hands, identify each type of thumb set you see. After you've identified the thumbs by type, look for the highest-rising, longest thumb you can find. You can use this person as a poster child for the Snorkeler viewpoint, the person who must go everywhere, must see everything. Next, look for the person with a thumb that's set quite low on the palm—the Scuba Diver. Since he is all about intensity and a passionate quest for the unusual, go ahead and say to him: "Wow, here's one for the dark side! You must have a very, very interesting private life." He will be astonished.

Finally, look for someone who has a thumb that ends midway between the heights reached by the Snorkeler and the depths explored by the Scuba Diver. This is your Swimmer. Tell her that her life is highlighted by phases. That she has periods when she will make sudden (and fairly radical) changes in her life directions. Sometimes this will take the form of leaving behind a tight circle of friends and associating with an entirely different set of people, having adventures that she would not have thought possible (or even desirable) in her previous incarnation. Reassure her that these phases are rarely permanent, but that they must be undertaken to satisfy interest and curiosity.

# Tag Along with Two Twenty-First-Century Palm Readers

Nothing compares with looking at palms in the real world, seeing the truly mind-bogglingly infinite differences among human beings. At the events where we read palms, we'll occasionally find people who are absolute spot-on examples of one of the thumb types. At one corporate event, a well-dressed man in an expensively tailored suit held up a palm with a particularly long, high-set thumb toward Sheila. Her response to him was immediate: "Is the Lear jet waiting out in the parking lot?" His astonished companions immediately broke out in loud laughter. This man was a very successful CEO of an up-and-coming sports clothing concern. He spent nine months a year globe-hopping in pursuit of worldwide success for his business. He was a Snorkeler to the core.

At these events we enjoy asking questions. Do Snorkelers socialize with Scuba Divers? Do Snorkelers marry each other or do they find partners mostly among Scuba Divers? Or Swimmers? Part of our work is exploring the connections between the personalities we encounter through palm reading. We've found that, in general, the different thumb sets tend to flock together. Most frequently in a tight-knit group of friends, you'll find Snorkelers with other

Snorkelers, Scuba Divers with other Scuba Divers. It's natural for us to find comfort with like-minded people—we'll be understood, we'll share values. The idea that like socializes with like is closer to what older books on palmistry would have you believe about the way the world works. Old-style palmistry is influenced mightily by the world of the Middle Ages, a world that was exceedingly hierarchical and where someone born to nobility was likely to stay a noble (barring disaster), and where a serf was bound to remain a serf (barring a miracle). However, where the old-style palmistry interpretations fall apart is in the sphere of romance. Passionate romance is no respecter of boundaries. In terms of relationships, you'll find the widest possible mix. Some of the most unlikely combinations will positively thrive as each other's one and only.

And there are exceptions in nonromantic relationships, as well. At one event, we met a woman with arresting dark eyes and dark hair. She had a very low set thumb. A real Scuba Diver. Sheila told her: "No one can tell you how to run your life. You *have* to see for yourself." Her friends (all Snorkelers!) screamed. Just by looking at the thumb, Sheila had uncovered the characteristic that distinguished this woman from her friends.

Once you learn how to identify the Swimmers, Snorkelers, and Scuba Divers in your life, friends will be clamoring for more of your "handy" insights.

# Lookers and Leapers

The thumb is all about making and carrying out decisions. When asked to give your judgment on a particular plan, you give the thumbs-up sign or you turn your thumb toward the floor. We modern palm readers look at the thumb as an indicator of the ways people make their choices and how they deal with those choices once they've made them. Give yourself the thumbs-up sign. Do this with your dominant hand (the one you sign checks with).

Now, hold that pose.

Look at the top part of your thumb, the part that extends from your thumbnail to your first knuckle. This part of your thumb is called the first phalange. In twenty-first-century palmistry, the top phalange represents human willpower. The will is that all-important part of our human selves that serves as the source of our energy, the part of us that puts into practice the decisions we make. What you see below the top phalange, this lower part of your thumb, is called (of course) the bottom phalange. The bottom phalange of your thumb is about reasoning power, the way each of us uses our imagination and intellect to make our decisions. The bottom phalange concerns itself with weighing and balancing, comparing and contrasting. The bottom phalange represents the kinds of questions that we frequently ask ourselves: Can we live with a choice we are about to make? Does the choice make sense? Should we act now? Or wait? This kind of reasoning is the province of the bottom phalange.

In trying to identify Swimmers, Snorkelers, and Scuba Divers, we looked at whether the thumb was set low or high on the palm. In determining whether we (or those close to us) are Lookers or Leapers, we look at the relative length of the top phalange and bottom phalange.

If you're a **Leaper,** the top part of your thumb is longer than the bottom part of the

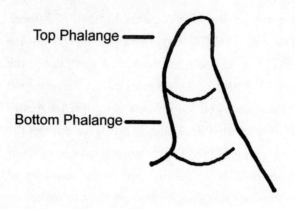

thumb. If you're a **Looker,** the bottom part of your thumb is longer than the top part of your thumb.

# Leapers

Let's take a close look at the top phalange.

For Leapers the top phalange is prominent, usually dwarfing the bottom phalange; it tells the twenty-first-century palm reader that this person is the possessor of abundant willpower. When the hand shows us an abundance of any quality—charm, logic, energy—we know we'll find evidence for it in the person's life. With Leapers, this is especially true.

Those who possess prominent top phalanges are called Leapers because they use willpower decisively and frequently. It often appears they leap into every project, always biting off more in any given time period than most other human beings do in their lifetimes. Planning is for slowpokes; if you're a Leaper, you've got a lot of willpower and the energy that drives the will. And you intend to use it.

Leapers tend to be the early adopters, those people who are up and riding the wave of the next big thing before the rest of us even know something new is shaking down at the beach. Successful Leapers make their decisions not by careful and deliberate preparation and pondering of the variables but by instinct and intuition. Leapers may later, after the dust has cleared, rationalize their choices, explaining them in a more methodical manner; but their choices are generated in the engine of the will, by a spark that becomes a decision to be acted on *immediately.*

While most people approach decisions with a certain amount of trepidation and uneasiness (this could *really* affect my life, best be careful) Leapers tend to display a genuine zest in their decision making, the way a marathon runner receives an endorphin high from using her well-trained muscles during a race.

Because they follow their gut instinct in making decisions and make decisions quickly and frequently, Leapers can get a reputation for being extremely flexible or confident. More cautious folks will often seek out Leapers when faced with truly difficult decisions, attracted by the confidence of these willful people.

For the Leaper, life is wonderful, *absolutely* wonderful, as long as his gut instincts are right. When he's right, well, he's one of the first in line (he bought Amazon before it split!). He's way ahead of the pack, reaping the early profits. As part of the vanguard, Leapers find themselves patting themselves on the back and looking around for other worlds to conquer, other opportunities to move the earth with their abundant willpower. If Leapers always made the right decisions, instantly, with nothing more than a feeling of deep excitement and inner certainty to guide them, life would be simple for them, and the rest of the world (with smaller, less impressive top phalanges) would envy them. And sigh. Wistfully.

However, Leapers are like everyone else; they're frequently wrong. They bet on the wrong pony, stock, or company. And they must live with the consequences. But unlike others, Leapers deal with their decisions in a very different and decidedly Leaper-ish manner. When Leapers make a wrong decision, they find themselves downstream a mile or two, all by themselves. It is part of the Leaper character that, however unpleasant the circumstances, she'll be paddling like crazy, even as the waters around her grow more turbulent and the circumstances more problematic. At this point, a great many non-Leapers would come to the conclusion that this is not working out, because it isn't. Most people would say, "Bad decision. I can't live with this. Time to renegotiate."

Most people. But *not* the Leaper.

With their abundant willpower, Leapers are always convinced that there is a chance that things will, quite magically, work out in some mysterious and unpredictable way. Long after Elvis has left the building, the klaxons are sounding, and a voice over the loudspeaker is announcing, "Twenty seconds to ship self-destruct," Leapers are convinced that the sky will clear and the true wisdom of their decision-making genius will be revealed. Remember, Leapers are possessed of a mighty will and the desire to use that will. They'll keep paddling, long, long after others have beached their canoes. They tell themselves: "I made my decision; I'm just going to have to live with it."

Because of their willpower, Leapers often have issues surrounding responsibility.

## Lookers

Assume the position.

That's right, give yourself a thumbs up, as we take a careful look at the bottom phalange to determine whether or not you are a Looker. If you're a Looker, you'll find that your bottom phalange is longer, more dominant than the top phalange. This bottom phalange is about reasoning, a person's personal style of sorting out the choices they make in life. The longer this section of your thumb, the more focus (and time) you will take working your way through the choices you make, all the choices—from what top to wear to work in the morning, to whom you will become romantically involved with. The key-word for the Looker perspective is *discrimination*. While Leapers pride themselves on being first in the water at the beach, Lookers will find the best and *perfect* place before they set down the towel and dip their feet into the water.

Lookers are life's master planners. They like to plan everything before making any commitments and agreeing to a course of action. Many people are driven to be cautious with decisions because they feel a deep need to make the *right* decision, and they're afraid if they make a wrong decision, they might not get a second chance.

This is not what motivates a Looker.

Lookers take time in the decision-making process, not out of fear but out of a positive affection for that process. Lookers seem to have an actual love for exploring possibilities, the mights and could be's of life. Most treat decisions like hot potatoes; they want to get them off of their hands as soon as humanly possible. Not so, Lookers. Their approach to decision making is leisurely. And, to a Leaper, sometimes exasperating. The Lookers' devotion to taking time to decide can drive the rest of humanity finally and completely to the bughouse. Which inspires us to utter a most serious word of advice: Leapers should *never* go shopping with Lookers.

Lookers will try on every shoe in the shoe store, drive every car on the car lot, and that's just for starters. Lookers shop, shop, shop, researching every *possible* option and outcome, driving their Leaper friends and partners wonderfully and absolutely nuts in the process. And if it's a truly major purchase, like a house, a Looker will weigh the options until doomsday and beyond. At last year's Microsoft picnic, Sheila read the palm of an uber-Looker. His significant other told us he had dragged her to *nineteen* different car dealerships before finally deciding on a Volkswagen Golf. While she shook her head in an advanced state of exasperation, our Looker smiled with satisfaction. As a Looker he'd exercised his decision-making duties admirably.

Lookers are excellent at improvising, and they *always* have a contingency plan. Because they're good at planning and organizing, they often get called in by both friends and relatives to clean up messes (although they're so organized, they very rarely create them).

> ### *Palms Up!* Prescription
> Lookers, be careful of saying yes! to every call for your troubleshooting skills; you have just so much energy. Since you're very good at cleaning up, organizing, and putting order to chaos, if you don't learn to say no, you'll never get a moment's rest in this world.

Lookers can be truly great strategists. They'll take the time to assess the options, the wrinkles that determine the success of any campaign. And although this thoroughness and attention to detail will often drive the Leapers to fits of frustration, it will also ensure the long-term health and success of a project.

Lookers also tend to be truth-tellers. Don't ask one for an opinion, unless you want to hear his viewpoint. Why? Because he'll give you his perspective in straightforward and, need I say, *detailed* terms. Lookers will often save Leapers from their folly; they can put even the most wayward train back on its tracks.

# The Leaper–Looker Combo

Occasionally, when we're performing, we'll come across a thumb that we call the dangerous combo. This is a thumb that has both a long top and a long bottom phalange: these people are both Leapers and Lookers. We always warn people: Never make anyone possessing this dangerous combo mad.

Why? Because the Leaper–Looker combination is truly formidable. Should you run afoul of these people, they not only have the willpower to quickly decide on taking revenge but also the patience, persistence, and practicality to construct a truly diabolical vengeance. Many successful people possessing this quality of implacable will and patience and thorough reasoning ability find their home in the legal profession.

# The Agatha Christie Thumb

A characteristic of modern-day palmistry is its attempt to blow away the dust and cobwebs from the folklore surrounding the art and science of palm reading. Once you begin to study old tomes of this art, you'll find murkiness in the way that palm readers of the past have dealt with some of the rarer features found in the human hand. A case in point is the Agatha Christie thumb. In old-school palmistry books, you'll see a formation called the *Murderer's Thumb,* and texts will make it sound as if its owner had his or her feet on the fast track to the gallows. This misinformation has not served to identify *any* criminal types but has made a few nice, sensitive folk feel bad. I hope it goes without saying that this kind of ill-considered name calling is part of the old-school palmistry we are dedicated to clearing up.

What does the Agatha Christie thumb look like? This thumb is unusual in that the top phalange comes in a large industrial size, which many palm readers logically read as a large (even an overabundance) of willpower. Like most features that are uncommon or unusual, there is a tendency for people to either overpraise it or be frightened of it. But the truth is that people with the Agatha Christie thumb display a truly relentless and roving thirst for finding a deep meaning in life. They are almost always fearless in this pursuit, and it forms a significant part of their lives. Many of us think about the mysteries of life, but these folks will go there, without a second thought.

When will is available in true abundance, it doesn't look like willpower anymore. Why? Because for most, willpower is associated with a certain amount of effort. We have to *try*, have to *push* a bit against whatever forces resist us. But in a situation of abundance, will is less effortful and, therefore, more comfortable about itself. Possessors of the Agatha Christie thumb are hard to intimidate, not because they are unyielding, full of themselves, or stubborn in any usual sense of the word. Instead, their storehouse of will is so large it's hard to make them feel challenged. They never consider the possibility of nonsuccess, even in a situation in which evidence of failure is staring them in the face. The Agatha Christie thumb is rare. When you're practicing your palmistry skills, look for it, and see if this interpretation doesn't make much more sense than the older takes on this thumb type.

# The Thumb Speaks: Who Is Stubborn?

When reading palms, especially at universities and colleges, we always ask people whether they're curious about who is absolutely, hands-down, the most stubborn person in the group. People usually *are* curious. Especially couples.

Why couples? Because couples, particularly those who've been in a relationship for any length of time, have their own sneaking suspicions about what's up in this very personal area, and they want outside confirmation of these musings.

To find the most stubborn person in a room, take the tip of each thumb and bend it back (very gently!). Some thumbs have no give at all. In fact,

some thumbs feel like the knuckle joint has calci-
fied to the extent that the entire thumb is made
up of a solid piece.

When you locate this type of thumb, one with
absolutely no give at the first knuckle, you've
found the most stubborn person in the room,
someone with a gift for saying no. These people
have an absolute facility in using the no-word, a
quality that some sociologists say is becoming
rarer and rarer in our culture. People with this
thumb quality have an exquisite sense of boundaries and usually extend this awareness to those
around them. If you ask them for something
they are not willing to give, they say (and mean)
no, clearly and unequivocally.

They make true and loyal friends. Should
you get in a scrape and find that you need their
support, they will stand shoulder to shoulder
with you regardless of the odds. They can also
be unbelievably stubborn, because when they've
made their minds up, that mind is well and
truly set.

On the other hand, if you find a thumb with
an easy and flexible top phalange, one you can

bend back with almost no effort, you have found a yes thumb.

Children of all ages love the possessors of such thumbs. The yes thumb is always willing to read that story one more time or stop by the toy store for a quick look at the latest diversions. Yes thumbs make wonderful parents and great companions. And, of course, flexibility is one of their keynotes.

# The Very Generous Thumb

Want to figure out whether the host of the next party you attend is going to start turning off the lights when the midnight hour comes or let the good times roll on and on? Have everyone hold his hand straight at you. And then (ever so gently) take a thumb in your right hand and, without applying any pressure, see how far out and down the thumb comes, without forcing, easily and naturally. If the thumb comes out easily to a ninety-degree angle (making a fairly credible L shape) then you'll be staying all night at this person's next party and probably sleeping on the most comfortable piece of furniture her living room contains.

If the thumb resists your gentle attempts to move it, then you should plan to be well behaved at the midnight hour, as you're escorted to the door with a firm (but loving) hand to find your way back home.

# The Thumb—Always a Good Place to Start

For new palm readers, the mighty thumb is an excellent place to start developing and refining your palmistry skills. As the icebreaker, start by telling someone whether he is a Swimmer, Snorkeler, or a Scuba Diver. Then determine whether he is a Leaper or a Looker. As you continue to read thumbs and palms, you'll get a feel for how other factors in the hand accentuate or deemphasize factors you've located in the thumb.

If you're comfortable being the center of attention at a party, there's no better place to start; and reading thumbs at a party *will* make you the center of attention!

# The Rest of the Digits

The fingers reveal a personality in general, and how that personality deals with making decisions. In this chapter we'll provide you with an overview of how the fingers fit into palmistry's big picture. You'll learn the secret of making personality assessments by observing the way certain fingers either do or do not cling together. We'll also reveal to you what the various fingers tell us about someone's self-image, values, strengths, and weaknesses.

# The Index Finger

Let's start with the index finger. The index finger (your "pointing finger") is known by old-school palm readers as the Jupiter finger, because they identified this finger with the father of the gods. (In Napoleon's time, palm readers in the City of Lights began to refer to this finger as the Napoleon finger to indicate their approval and support for the most powerful person they could think of who regularly consulted a palm reader.) No matter what you call it, the index finger is about our public selves—our jobs, what we do for a living, how we make our way in the world. This public self represented by the index finger is often the part of ourselves that our friends know best. The index finger has three parts, called, as we have learned, phalanges. The length of each phalange can tell you important details about the personality of the person whose palm you are reading. Here's a quick look at each of the phalanges and what they stand for.

# The Top Phalange

The top phalange reveals how a person makes meaning of their world. The older classics of palm reading call this the phalange of spirituality, but we have found it is as much about aesthetics and seeing meaningful patterns in the world around us as anything specifically religious.

# The Middle Phalange

In old-style books on palmistry, you'll find the middle phalange called the phalange of intellect, but it's far more than that. This phalange is not about being an intellectual, it is about using the mind to *do* things in the real world. While the top phalange is about the mind exploring the inner world, the middle phalange is the mind facing outward, looking for ways to make a difference in the lives we live.

# The Bottom Phalange

When we reach the bottom phalange, we are in the realm of the physical world. The physical world is about activity, about being active physically. This phalange tells us about how much emphasis a person will place on being—and doing things—in the world. For some, the physical world is the most important part of their reality; here they take into account what people do for them, the more actual, physical, the better. So the concerns of the bottom phalange are the concerns of the physical world, health, physical well-being, and daily activities.

## If the Top Phalange Is Longest

People whose top phalange of the index finger is noticeably longer than the other two are likely to find their life's meaning in their work, in their public activities, or in expressing themselves in a public context rather than in their private life. They are likely to find the most comfortable expression of themselves as politicians, entertainers, salespeople. They will derive active pleasure from being with and interacting with other people in their day-to-day life.

# If the Middle Phalange Is Longest

If the middle phalange of the index finger is the longest, then the public self is more likely to be involved with the world of doing things with the mind, the intellect. Ideas are going to be an important part of the currency in which this person trades. When dealing with someone who has a prominent middle phalange, it's important to remember that for her, thinking *is* doing. Middle phalange people tend to be somewhat driven and have very active mental lives.

*Palms Up!* **Prescription**

Middle phalange people may at times need to take radical vacations to keep their edge. People with this feature need to be very, very proactive about burnout. They can and do drive themselves harder than anyone else. They perform best when they actively schedule downtime.

# If the Bottom Phalange
# Is Longest

A large bottom phalange on the index finger is all about action and activity as the meaning of life (at least the public part of life). People with this feature use whatever energy they have to accomplish things. To those around them they appear to be working off some inner checklist, marking off accomplishments one at a time.

These are the kind of people, who, if you haven't seen them in a couple of months, and you ask them what they've done, they will reel off a series of activities and accomplishments—some large, some small—of near-boggling diversity. They see life in terms of projects, and if you talk to them for long, you will find them trying to involve you in one or to convince you to start one of your own.

# Who Is the Master Planner in the Room?

The easiest thing for the *Palms Up!* reader to tell about a person from their index finger is how much she likes to be the Master Planner in any situation. Master Planners are not necessarily pushy or dominating; in fact, they are often blessed with abundant charm—even charisma. They also possess extremely prominent index fingers.

How long is an extremely prominent index finger? In 99 percent of the hands you'll read, the middle finger will be the longest, most prominent finger. The index finger will reach, in almost all cases, to the bottom edge of the nail of the middle finger. If your index finger extends *beyond* where that nail starts, welcome to Master Planner territory. You prefer projects in which you have final-cut privileges, are able to hire and fire as you please, and sit down in the chair marked "Director."

Isn't that the way it's *supposed* to be?

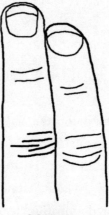

**Master
Planner**

# Team Players and Free Agents

The relationship of the index finger to the finger next to it, the middle finger, can also give us important information about its owner. In this section we'll look at two very different kinds of personalities, Team Players and Free Agents.

Here's how to tell which you are:

• If your index finger sticks close to your middle finger, you're a Team Player.

• If your index finger veers away radically from your middle finger, heading thumbward, you're a Free Agent.

• If your index finger, middle finger, and ring finger are equally spaced, you tend to be very flexible, able to work as part of a team when you need to, but also able to pull up stakes and negotiate for yourself as a Free Agent.

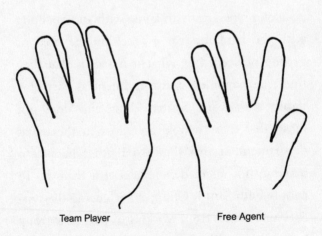

Team Player          Free Agent

# The Team Player

A person with an index finger closer to, or pointing toward, their middle finger (related in old-fashioned palmistry books to the planet Saturn) has what we call *Saturn Cling*. The middle finger and the index finger buddy up, sticking close to one another. People who have this feature find that they have their best, most exciting and satisfying work and encounters in public and professional life as a part of groups or teams. They are team players, and they spend much of their time and energy in life looking for the perfect group to belong to. This *doesn't* mean they are get-along go-along types, ready to agree with and go along with the herd for fear of rocking the boat or getting noticed. No, what it means is that they find true happiness and fulfillment as part of a tightly knit team. Saturn Cling also does not mean that these people are short in the talent department or that they need other people to make up for talent deficiencies. Far from it. To people with Saturn Cling, experiencing the synergy that comes from working as part of a group is the ultimate thrill.

# The Free Agent

If the person's index finger veers away from the middle finger—in fact if it heads away from all the other fingers, heading to the thumb—then he's a Free Agent. Those who have such an index finger either do something unusual for a living, or do something that everyone else does but in some unusual way. People with this wandering index finger are self-starters; they pick the projects they do, not to please the crowd or the people they work with, but to please themselves. Free Agents often feel propelled through life by what amounts to a personal destiny—not destiny with a capital *D*—but by a sense that an inner need empowers them to do the public things they involve themselves in. Free Agents are usually happiest in professions that allow them to make the personal public. They work hard to realize their personal vision, and they won't be doing it for their group or team but to satisfy some need deep within, a way of working out their personal destiny and private vision. Right now, with technology transforming the world so rapidly and whole new professions coming into existence in an eye blink, the world seems especially ripe for Free Agents.

# How Does It Relate?

When you are reading palms, we encourage you to look for *relationships*—not only on the romantic side of life but between the fingers on the hands you are examining. Let's start learning to see these relationships by looking at your own hand. Unfold your palm and take a good close look at how long your index finger is compared to your ring finger.

If your index finger is longer than your ring finger, think David Geffen, a person able to take talent and represent it to the world; he's the quintessential agent. People with long index fingers tend to have advanced skills in the art of schmoozing, negotiating, presentation, and dynamic compromise—all of the elements at play in the dealmaker's art. Agents are famous for counting the cost and asking for the green up front. Agents expect to get paid for the work they do and are unashamed and unsentimental about negotiating their cut. They can be astonishingly and breathtakingly down to earth about negotiations, and at the end of a project, when the spreadsheets are run, the hours worked *always* equal the dollars paid.

What happens when your ring finger (the finger of art; more on this finger soon!) is longer than your index finger (the finger of business)? When you have this combination, you're having a love affair with the creative side; and, like all people in love, you rarely (if ever) count the cost. When you're deeply in love, business is the very *last* thing on your mind. On any project that you become involved in, you will throw your whole self into it, focusing all of your talents and resources on the matter at hand. Hours, days, even months later when you emerge from the cave where you've been wrestling with your project, should you run the spreadsheet to determine your dollar-per-hour wage on the project, you'll find that your actual pay (for the time, tears, and brain cells you've lavished on your creative act) is abysmally low. Have you even managed minimum wage? If your ring finger outstrips your index finger, you don't really care.

> ### *Palms Up!* Prescription
>
> If you're the proud possessor of a ring finger that's longer than your index finger, look around for a person in your general vicinity who has that long index finger to share his agent talent with you. Beg him to teach you the financially wise ways of the agent breed. Many talent-heavy individuals can be helped to a healthier (and happier) lifestyle by taking some inspiration and lessons from those with the agent finger.

If your index finger rivals the middle finger in length, you tend to be generous and love to give (as well as to receive) gifts. Because of their love of (and almost addiction to) prodigality, people with this trait may have to learn to limit their generosity, sticking to a budget, giving only *one* party a month, or sticking to a certain dollar amount for the gifts they give. Since, for you, giving parties just plain feels good, you probably entertain quite often, inviting people over for a get-together.

# The Middle Finger

In the old books on palmistry, you'll find the middle finger associated with Saturn, a law giver and a stern judge. This accounts for the finger's reputation for severity, for austerity and darkness. But the truth about this finger is more complicated, more subtle. The middle finger is really about community, what we owe to the communities we're a part of. The middle finger is concerned with the way we make ourselves a part of the greater whole, the web of relationships that make up our lives. The middle finger is also about traditions, about the customs and laws we establish as human beings to make our world work; it's about duty, with a capital *D*. This, after all, is the glue that holds our relationships and our social universe together.

So, in our culture, the middle finger is usually about one thing: guilt. The middle finger is at the center of the hand and (in almost all cases) is the longest of the fingers. Its very position gives it an important role to a play in the personal world. If the index finger is about the face that people present to the world, the middle finger is about the way they see (and judge) themselves in relation to their world and the community and groups they belong to. Think of the middle finger as everyone's very own personal and private critique of both the private and the public self. Very much like Freud's superego.

The superego, legend has it (no one has ever captured one in the wild, tagged it, weighed it, and released it), is that parental part of the mind, perpetually busy bringing us up on charges like some insubstantial but very vocal district attorney. To the superego, we never quite measure up. Perhaps (according to it) we never will.

Old-school books on palmistry don't spend a lot of time on the middle finger, probably because it was considered such a dark subject. But we take a different (and, we hope, lighter) look at this important finger. Like many of our deepest concerns, once you share a double-latte with it at your local Starbucks, get some hang time with it, the fear factor goes way, way down.

# "The Finger"

The use of the middle finger as a means to show anger and rebellion is at least as old as ancient Greece. Although there's no evidence that Socrates ever gave anyone the finger, the gesture was in use during his lifetime, three hundred years before the birth of Christ. In the ages since, giving the finger has become the classic way to show extreme disapproval. When you wish to tell someone off, flashing her this simple sign tells her instantly and emphatically that you have excluded her from your community, your social world. Simple and elegant, the middle finger lets everyone know that the social contract between you and the individual you've pointed at has completely broken down.

For *Palms Up!* palm readers this should make you aware of both the light and the dark side of the digit, its basic power. Although the finger is the most famous (and common) use of a single digit to send a message, it's good to remember that *all* the fingers of the hand have the same potential power to signal deep emotion.

# The Community Finger and Responsibility

Because the middle finger is about responsibility and duty, many people are uncomfortable with some of the concepts it represents. Some people don't even like the sound of the word *responsibility*. It's a word that grabs most of us by the guilt handles and pulls hard. Are we giving enough to our family? Our friends? The people we work with? Our romantic other? Too many people, it seems, can be easily manipulated by the people they're closest to, the ones they love and care about the most, by a few well-chosen and well-timed words. Responsibility is the way they both consciously and unconsciously order their priorities and values.

When looking at the middle finger, take care to see how this longest finger looks in relation to the fingers on either side. In most cases you'll find the index finger and the ring finger end just beneath where the fingertip of the middle finger begins. Here are some things to look for:

- If the middle finger is much longer than the two fingers beside it, you can expect the person to be concerned with issues that affect his home community. Pure water and good school systems are issues that can gather and keep the attention of those with longer middle fingers, because these public issues matter.

• If the middle finger is much shorter than the two fingers beside it, expect the person to be less driven by the outside world than by the internal, personal world. Private issues concerning people closest to him will matter most.

# The Community Finger's Phalanges

The phalanges of the middle finger can tell us what kind of spin the individual whose hand we are reading puts on the ideas of community, duty, and responsibility as she works through them in her life. In this section we'll look at the top, middle, and bottom phalanges of your middle finger. As we do so, we'll be interpreting the way you as an individual handle the concepts of community and duty. The longer each phalange on the middle finger is, the more of certain qualities you will possess. Let's take a look.

## When the Top Phalange Is Longest

Let's look at your middle finger. Hold it up vertically in front of your face in a relaxed manner. Look carefully and ask yourself, which one of the phalanges is the longest? If the top phalange (the one that includes the fingernail) is longest, ask a second question: What is the effect when the largest phalange on your finger of community and duty is the one having to do with spirituality and meaning making? If the top phalange of your middle finger is longer than the lower two, your sense of duty and community will be driven by a profound need to see the big picture in terms of the groups of which you're a part, and you'll find your greatest happiness and satisfaction seeking (and speaking) meaning for the group of which you are a part.

Georgia O'Keefe is a good example of an individual who as an artist became the voice of something larger. In pictures taken of her by the photographer Alfred Stieglitz, you can see the prominent top phalange of O'Keefe's middle finger. Although an intensely private individual, O'Keefe's work as an artist embodies a quality that goes far beyond her as a person and speaks to all women artists who came after her. People with a long top phalange tend to find their greatest satisfactions when they speak for a group or cause that is larger than their singular selves. They also find it very difficult to comprehend or appreciate those who put themselves first or whose greatest goal in life is chasing mere wealth or creature comforts.

## When the Middle Phalange Is Longest

If you notice that the middle section of your Saturn finger is larger than the other two phalanges, then your approach to duty and community is centered on the intellect. The middle phalange is about the world of the human mind, about invention, about the ideas that are transforming the world in which we live, and the way we live in that world. To those with a large middle phalange on your middle finger, intellectual property is *not* just an abstraction, an esoteric concern designed exclusively to provide patent attorneys a living and software companies a battlefield. Here's the way to think about it: Brilliant ideas are often called brainchilds, and—consciously or unconsciously—that's the way people with this characteristic think and *feel*. To steal the ideas of this person is to take and misuse a part of his very self. You have a passion for ideas, and you deeply believe that ideas are a way to bring value to your community. This passion often means that you will form alliances with political or social groups that want to bring benefit to the community. You feel that an important, even crucial part of life (need we say—a *duty?*) is to do your bit in the world by bringing good ideas to those around you. This passion for ideas makes you a wonderful conversationalist and dinner companion.

## When the Bottom Phalange Is Longest

When the bottom phalange of your middle finger is the longest, you are a straight shooter and somewhat skeptical about believing the things your fellow human beings say. The bottom phalange is all about action, about doing real things in the real world. When this characteristic is married to the world of community and duty represented by the Saturn finger, the result is someone who does not listen so much to what people *say* but watches what they *do*. Straight shooters furnish their relationships with loyalty. You are wonderfully dependable. When all of your friends have forgotten someone's birthday, you—with your long lower phalange—will show up with a cupcake and some candles to bail him out. The very worst thing someone can do to a straight shooter is make a promise and then break it. Although many people are loose with their promises, straight shooters never are. Straight shooters also tend to be very good judges of character, because they pay more attention to what people do than to what they say. Because of this tendency to take what people say with more than a grain of salt, you do well in professions like law enforcement, where it is important—even crucial—to view the words of others with large amounts of skepticism.

As a straight shooter you put people through a kind of trial period before you let them permanently inside your life and allow them to become a friend. You do not assume that a friendship exists just because you've attended a few parties at each other's houses, enjoyed frequent conversations with one another, or have a taste for the same movies or music. Straight shooters must wait, will wait, until enough actions in the real world have accumulated to reveal a true friendship. Once you've made that determination, you'll be there for your friend, no matter what vicissitudes life throws your way.

And, of course, you expect your friends to be there for you as well. If you're one of those people who like relationships to come with no strings, a relationship with a straight shooter will not be your cup of tea. When it comes to relationships, straight shooters take their responsibilities seriously. You will often behave as if there were an unspoken agreement between the two of you when it comes to the responsibilities of friendship—whether you've talked it over together or not. This can be disconcerting for people with a relaxed, laissez faire attitude toward relationships. Yes, you will be there for a friend should Hurricane Elsie take his house away into a storm-whipped sky; but you'll be deeply chagrined if he does not return the favor in like circumstances.

## What If All My Phalanges Are Equal?

Although it's rare, some people have almost identically sized phalanges. If this is you, you have both a keen sense of self and a deep sense of community. Because, much more than most, you are able to work comfortably and creatively with these two sometimes tricky areas of life, you will make a wonderful negotiator. You tend to be cool headed during upsets in the communities you are a member of and never lose sight of the way that differences in viewpoints frequently make a group strong. When others are ferociously set on getting accommodation for their viewpoint and allegiances, you—being a more balanced individual— are able to remind them that winning does not always solve problems. If your phalanges are equal, you are often able to smooth ruffled feathers and help others find powerful compromises that benefit everyone—not just a few.

# The Middle Finger and Fingertips

Since the Saturn finger is all about community and duty, when you're checking out a significant other's middle digit, you'll want to take a careful look at her fingertips. This'll tell you the way she thinks about *and* activates her sense of duty and honor in relationships.

Shall we start with ourselves? Hold your hand out in front of your face, with your palm facing *away* from you. You should be able to see your knuckles and your fingernails. We are going to take a look at the shape of your fingertips and assess what these shapes say about the way you deploy the twin forces of duty and community in your life—your own personal relationship style.

## Pointed Fingertips

If you've got a pointed fingertip on your Saturn finger, your approach to duty and community is creative, expressive, and meaning oriented, rather than practical. Imagination is a hallmark of your approach to duty. In this age of the Internet, personal cellular devices, and broadband home access, people with pointed Saturn fingers have a more natural, more intuitive sense of this web of relationships. Pointed Saturn finger people have a feel for community. Along with the ability to sense human connectedness, you will also have a sense of duty that is expressive. You become especially creative during holidays, often making presents for others.

## Rounded Fingertips

Rounded fingertips speak of bringing disparate people and ideas together. If yours are rounded fingertips, you're about entrepreneurship and diplomacy. There is creativity aplenty in rounded fingertips, but also an urge toward mediation, to bringing people together—active diplomacy. What is active diplomacy? While pointed fingers can be fairly self-contained, and even self-involved at times, you love (and to some extent *need*) the back and forth that comes with dealing and negotiating with other people. For you, duty and community are dealt with actively, by bringing people together for a common purpose. You are likely to be a member of the Chamber of Commerce or to root for the home team. Rounded nails on the middle finger also indicate that you have the ability to get along naturally and easily with many kinds of people.

## Square Fingertips

If you have square fingertips on the middle finger you deal with community and duty by taking action. You believe that relationships between groups of people are created only by the back and forth of constant activity in real time. You are not interested in holidays for religious or cultural reasons but because they pull people together—and this working together is what creates healthy communities. The creativity and expressiveness found in people with pointed or rounded fingertips will seem overly theoretical to square fingertip types.

To people with square fingertips on their middle fingers, the joy of duty and community is best celebrated by the modern equivalent of a barn raising: helping a friend move or paint a room in his house. You show up to volunteer a hand (or a paintbrush) when someone is moving across town into a new house. And if he wants you to remain his true friend, he'll show up when you need help.

You, with your square fingertips, know when to put the spurs to a project. You know how to crack the whip when it's necessary, and your focus is infectious. You do not have to be persuaded to get on task when you are working as part of a group with a goal. You were born that way.

You will raise the activity level of any group you become a part of, but you can sometimes be perceived as a hard taskmaster by those around you, who are less focused and possess less of the nose-to-the-grindstone attitude.

# The Ring Finger

In palmistry the ring finger—the Apollo finger—is the finger of art and creativity. The ring finger represents self-expression, the arts, and the countless ways we conspire with our brain's right and left hemispheres to see and make meaning out of the world we live in and the lives we lead in that world. Because the making of meaning is grounded by this finger, it is also about our modern sense of spirituality.

The first thing to notice when assessing the art finger is how long it is in relationship to the fingers around it. Although in our humble opinion, there is *no such thing* as a completely normal human being, in about 80 percent of people the ring finger ends where the nail of the middle finger begins. You'll find this to be true in most cases. But we've read the hands of thousands of individuals, and we've never come close to identifying an absolutely *average* human hand—so prepare yourself for some surprises. With that said, a good starting point for gauging the prominence of Apollo (the finger of art) in someone's life is whether the ring finger is longer or shorter, compared to the cuticle of the middle finger. Then notice the length of the three phalanges. The top phalange is related to holistic, even visionary, thinking, while the middle and bottom phalanges have to do with the intellectual and the physical realms of creativity.

## A Long Top Phalange

If the first section of your ring finger is longer than the other two phalanges, your creativity will take a visionary (and sometimes radically visual) bent. Creativity and emotion will be more than just well balanced; they will be in constant interplay, and you will possess a kind of creativity that allows you to view life in radical ways, different from those around you. We call this type of person a Da Vinci, after Leonardo Da Vinci, whose career was informed by a restless and far-seeing creativity.

Da Vincis will actively look for opportunities to infuse every waking moment with the new, the novel. There is a restlessness about you, an always-moving quality that can sometimes wear out those around you. You can be a notable visionary, taking a big picture view of the world around you. While most people see and are involved in the day-to-day details of their lives, the possessor of a long top phalange on the ring finger will have the ability to see the entire landscape in the area of her expertise.

Da Vincis are the great mavericks of life, lending color, creativity, and depth to every project they come into contact with and every relationship they're involved with. You specialize in seeing the world in unusual ways. Where other people see a field of stones, Da Vincis visualize the buildings, the neighborhoods, the cities that will rise from the pebble-strewn expanse.

If you have a relationship with a Da Vinci, prepare yourself for and expect constant—and often radical—change to be a part of your life. Da Vincis are easily bored; they're happiest when their careers are changing, offering levels of novelty that others might consider overwhelming. Although a relationship with a Da Vinci can be hectic, it's never boring.

Remember, Da Vincis are dedicated to creativity. Although other aspects of life are of interest to them, the reasons they focus on any particular area of life will be anything but typical. If a Da Vinci becomes interested in the world of finance, it will *not* be primarily or solely to amass Godzilla-size chunks of the folding green so she can retire to a privately owned Greek island, on which to while away her time and energy sampling fancy wines and working on her tan. No, the Da Vinci sees money as a kind of "green energy," part of a complex system of communication and value, a means of communication that's flexible and capable of serving as a vehicle of self-expression, as do the paints of a painter or the words of a skillful writer.

Da Vincis bring an (not just visual) artist's eye to everything they do. They are often metaphorical thinkers who see the world in metaphorical terms. A tree or an apple to these creative thinkers is never *just* a plant or a fruit. To the Da Vinci, a tree may be the great tree of life—a symbol of our genetic heritage, the dance of DNA self-expressing through species and individuals. Does this give you a feel for the kind of thinking that is second nature to the Da Vinci?

As a *Palms Up!* reader, remember that the artistic and the spiritual are deeply linked beneath the surface. In assessing the impact of the finger of art, recall that art and an attraction to the artistic are about making meaning of the always mysterious world. Because of this, Da Vincis are especially capable as speakers for spiritual concepts and especially the value of creativity.

Since the top phalange of the ring finger is all about finding the meaning of life through creativity, Da Vincis see the value of life in terms of creativity and little else. While some may look at public figures like Donald Trump and Bill Gates in terms of the material possessions these two earthlings have amassed, Da Vincis look at (and evaluate) these two fellow human beings in terms of their creativity.

If you're a Da Vinci, your heroes, the people you admire, will most likely be creative types, performers of all types: rock stars, actors, painters, musicians, philosophers. Even if the people you admire come from the world of business, you will tend to admire them for the creative side of their endeavor rather than their sheer financial clout. And how much creativity, how much vision, does it take to be the leader of a corporation like Microsoft, the most successful corporation that has ever existed? How much creativity do you need to steer a financial empire like Donald Trump? Answer: plenty. In the world of science, imagine the creativity of an Albert Einstein or a Neils Bohr.

This emphasis, this *insistence,* on creativity as the basis of life makes the Da Vinci wildly entertaining and an inspiration to be around. In the midst of a life filled with everyday responsibilities and commitments here and appointments there, Da Vincis remind us that an underground river, the unconscious, flows beneath everything, at every minute of the night and day. They remind us that even the most quotidian moments in life arise out of this basic creative flow. Da Vincis are closer to this knowledge than the rest of humanity.

# A Long Second Phalange

If the second phalange of your ring finger is larger than the other two, you are the kind of person, like James Dean or the young Marlon Brando, who comes to define for a generation what it is to be an artist and a rebel—like Bono, the lead singer for U2. More than just a rock star and musician, Bono is an activist, screenplay writer, and general rebel. If you have a long second phalange on your ring finger, there will be a major intellectual component to your creativity. You are remarkable for cleverness and wit, for creative and intellectual mixing of sense and sensibility.

Bonos have major talents in the area of verbal skills. Humor (whether we acknowledge it as a major intellectual skill or not) is keynoted in these people. For Bonos, the mouth is a tool of creative self-expression. This makes them mesmerizing— if not always completely truthful—storytellers.

You are attracted to art that has an intellectual side. Art that makes you think . . . and talk. Most Bonos have at least considered becoming members of book clubs or discussion groups, because to you none of life's experiences can be thoroughly digested without equal amounts of conversation and meditation on meaning. While some people can experience art emotionally or spiritually and be quite satisfied with the experience, you feel you must delve further.

# A Long Bottom Phalange

If the bottom phalange of your ring finger is the longest of your phalanges, then there is a decidedly physical side to your approach to art and self-expression. Our name for such an individual is a Jackie Chan.

The physical side of high art is represented by ballet and modern dance, but the physical side of human self-expression is not limited to the recognized and well-accepted art forms. Probably no one exemplifies this better than Jackie Chan. To the global audience, he is a bigger star than Tom Cruise or Jack Nicholson. His work in popular films shows us that with enough skill, humor, and focus, even Hong Kong action films can rise to the level of art. The incredible discipline and risk taking in his films speak directly to the human urge to transcend human limitations in the physical world. Anyone who has seen a Chan film knows there is an artistic side to physical self-expression. As a Jackie Chan, your desire is to make the physical spiritual. You take the flesh beyond the flesh, to something artistic and meaningful.

Dance itself has long been considered a fine, and sometimes sacred, art. But even painting and music (not necessarily art forms associated with physicality) can become very physical in the hands of some practitioners. Look at a painter like Jackson Pollack, one of the great radical painters of the twentieth century, a painter who attacked his canvases with an unequaled ferocity and physicality. Anyone who's seen *Number 1, 1950 (Lavender Mist)* is struck by the passionate density of the painting, its almost physical assault on the visual sense.

It may take on a variety of forms, but at heart the sensibility of a Jackie Chan turns physical activity into deep self-expression, into art. You like to show approval and appreciation in physical ways. At baseball games, you will be the one shouting the loudest, screaming when the umpire gets it wrong, rejoicing when the calls are going the home team's way. At the opera, you cry "Bravo!" at the top of your lungs.

Remember, the Apollo finger is all about the

interface between the emotions and the mind and about the way we make meaning out of the world. Jackie Chans express their meaning-finding sensibilities in physical terms. They become bored by art or artistic performances that are too much based in the head, too theoretical. They are drawn to works of art that percolate with movement, activity, and physicality. While Bonos may see chess as an art and might attend a chess match in which two titans of intellect sit across from one another in a room full of breathless anticipation, a room in which someone's clearing his throat is a hanging offense, Jackie Chans would rather die than be stuck in this audience.

## Leaning Toward Saturn

If your ring finger (the Apollo finger) leans toward your middle finger, you insist on having your creative powers serve the community, and you tend to put your creativity at the service of advancing group goals and commitments. No matter how large the group, you'll put your creativity to work on creating the sense of an extended family. People with ring fingers that lean toward the middle finger are often attracted to the holidays. They experience an almost religious buzz from ensuring that the traditions of Christmas are shining bright and green. They'll put all of their intense creativity into making sure that their Halloween costume will outshine the Addams family.

The kind of creativity these people will muster up is always very intelligible to their fellow citizens, very grounded, and easy to understand. That's the way Apollo leaning toward Saturn people prefer things to be. They display (for the most part) absolutely no appreciation for art that is abstract, purely intellectual, or created solely to please the person making it. For being surprisingly open-minded on so many subjects, they take a surprisingly dim view of art for art's sake.

# The Baby Finger

Time to meet the baby finger—a digit whose time has come.

The baby finger is the little guy, the runt of the litter. In the crowd of thumb, index, middle, and ring fingers, it gets a bit less noticed with all its taller siblings pushing forward in a demand for our attention and time. But now, it's the baby finger's turn. In *Palms Up!,* we give the baby finger its due.

The baby finger is all about communication. In times past, palm readers associated the little finger with Mercury, swift messenger of the gods, someone who could—at the speed of thought—carry messages from Olympus, where the gods were known to dwell, to us lucky humans on the mortal plane.

Take a look at your baby finger. Hold your hand out in front of your face so that your palm faces you. Relax your hand so that the fingers stretch out, but not so they become rigid and completely stiff. That's right, just relax . . . because the first thing we'll look at is, where is your little finger in relation to the other fingers?

## The Wanderer

Some people will see that the baby finger sticks out away from the other fingers, as if the other fingers are the herd, and the little finger is marching to a different tune. If that's the case, you're what we call a *Different Drummer.* You tend to be the slightest bit eccentric, possessing a high tolerance for individuality in others and yourself. You have the ability to not only create but also inhabit your own private (and somewhat secret) garden, usually from quite an early age. Different Drummers at times seem to be communicating in 6/8 time, while the rest of the crowd is busy keeping the beat in steady old dependable 4/4.

The good news for Different Drummers is that they are natural-born communicators. But often their best communication is with themselves, which can lead them to create and lead (mentally) a kind of secret life that even their significant others might be unaware of.

If you are a Different Drummer, you're going to spend at least some of your time giving your significant other clues to your mental and imaginative whereabouts. If you're a Different Drummer, might we give you some *Palms Up!* advice? We suggest that you make a habit of *regularly* giving those you're closest to accurate map coordinates to help them locate where you stand on the important issues, which can spell the difference between a run-of-the-mill relationship and one that keeps working and throwing off the kinds of sparks that provide both light and warmth.

For the Different Drummers, there's usually something unusual, something original about the way they communicate. They can be easily imitated and even caricatured because of the stylish way they communicate to the world outside their own skins.

If you are a Different Drummer, you have what we call maverick Mercury, so get ready for interesting side excursions in life. Be prepared for, and resigned to, the fact that your quicksilver nature is going to take you quite naturally to places, people, and ideas that other people might never think of visiting.

If you yourself don't have maverick Mercury, but you have a relationship with someone who possesses this trait, your life will *never* be humdrum while he is around.

# The Thinking Side
# of the Palm

The side of the hand that the baby finger dwells on is about Thinking with a capital *T*, not Doing with a capital *D*. And people with wandering Mercury can be very original thinkers and talkers. They find themselves attracted to unusual ideas and ways of thinking simply because they are original. The possessors of wandering Mercury make great salespeople, because they not only find it easy to form a romantic bond with ideas but also find themselves capable, even adept, at speaking the truths they've located in the world at large. And they have a natural flair for dramatizing those ideas and making them live for others.

For maverick Mercuries, thinking *is* traveling. They can go places mentally and be every bit as satisfied as the globe-hopper who maxes out her frequent flyer miles visiting faraway places with strange-sounding names. If you are a card-carrying member of the Maverick Mercury Society for a More Interesting Life, check out the travel lines on the edge of your palm—that's right, all the way over there on the edge. Imagine that you're giving a karate chop. The side of your hand that would do the striking—all the way from the base of your baby finger down to where the hand meets the wrist—is called the percussion. At the bottom of the percussion, close to the wrist, is where you'll find the travel lines. The deep ones are considered signs of trips that you will have little choice about, such as business travel; the finer lines indicate discretionary travel, trips that you will *choose* to take. These lines are especially important to you maverick Mercury types. Why? Because thinking and traveling just seem naturally to go together. And given opportunity, maverick Mercuries will go there and do that as frequently as the frequent-flyer miles allow.

## Sticking Close to Apollo

What if your baby finger shows a close relationship and affection for the ring finger (the finger of art)? Baby fingers that hug the ring finger are all about culture, refinement, and discernment. You speak of the civilizing influences: the well-lit room, the beautifully decorated interior space that indicates culture and sophistication. Your words are reasonable and measured. You're Bach to the Different Drummer's Beethoven. Besides revealing the way you communicate, the baby finger also speaks about risk taking: the style (and degree) of risk taking you like to involve yourself in. The baby finger tells us:

• What strategies a person will use to negotiate the risks he will find (and even seek out) in life.
• What flavors of risk he will have a positive appetite for.

## Long Baby Fingers

If you have a long baby finger, that is, one that reaches up past the bottom of the top phalange of the ring finger, you can be trusted with money because you are conservative in the handling of the green stuff. Not only can you be trusted with your own funds but also with others' money. The risks you take are well thought out. If you have a long baby finger, the risks you feel comfortable with are those that allow for calculation and preparation. You'll be fond of the risks associated with chess rather than those with the unpredictability (and house percentages) associated with craps. As a person with a long baby finger, you're perfectly willing to take risks—as long as you can take precise control of the variables.

You might be known for your gift of gab. The baby finger is about how you use your words in the act of communication. Your long baby finger means you could be a powerfully persuasive salesperson if you intellectually accept the concept behind the project or service. You love to talk. On long car trips you can drive other people crazy.

## Short Baby Fingers

If you have a short baby finger, one that does not rise up as far as the top of the bottom phalange of the ring finger, you're the kind of person who's more comfortable with risk than your fellow citizens. You frequently take risks for the things you believe in. You can be a bit brash and, certainly, more than a bit daring. You're apt to be impulsive and have a positive thirst for the kinds of experiences that produce toxic amounts of adrenaline in more timid folks. Along with this hunger for risk is usually a fairly obvious pride in the experiences you've managed to amass in your sweet, short life. You're very often the first person in your group to try the next big thing—whatever that might be. Extreme sports, bubble tea, the latest and greatest, you like to be there first and have the experience before other people have beat a nice, comfortable (and to you, boring) trail to it.

# The Palm

## The Life Line, the Head Line, the Heart Line, the Fate Line

Let's turn our attention now to the palm. The palm speaks to us about the particular, specific events that go into making up a life; it also speaks to us about certain general qualities. We're going to dispel some of the myths about the major lines of the hand: the Life Line, the Head Line, the Heart Line, and (cue the Chinese gong, please!) the Fate Line.

# Locating the Life Line

Looking down at the palm of your dominant hand (the one you sign autographs with!), you will see a line that begins between your thumb and the index finger; it travels in an arc across the palm, curving toward the wrist. This line, which creates a circle around the base of the thumb, is the Life Line. The Life Line shows some basic elements of our personalities: the level of vitality we have, and the intensity with which we live our lives. It reveals personality traits such as ambition, extraversion, or introversion. Of all the lines in the hand, none is better known than the Life Line. In our years of palm reading, we've found that people are more concerned about their Life Line than any other area of their palm. In fact some people will say, "You can read my palm—but *please* don't tell me anything about my Life Line." Why do they say this?

In the past, some palmists have spread the idea

that short Life Lines mean short lives. Let us take this opportunity to debunk that myth. Anyone who's practiced palm reading for a significant period of time knows that a short Life Line *does not* mean a short life. Never. Modern palm readers do not read the length of the Life Line as an indicator of length of life. We look at *depth* of

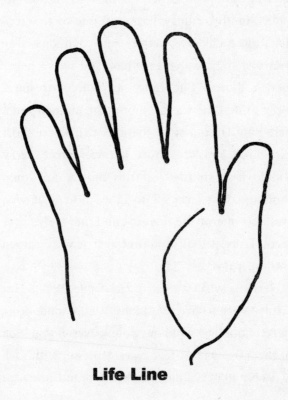

**Life Line**

line to tell us important things about a person's personality, approach to life, and attitude toward aging.

## The Hot Chile Pepper

One of the most memorable palms we've ever read was the palm of Jerry, which we did on his eighty-ninth birthday. Jerry was one of the liveliest, most talkative, active—and opinionated—human beings we've ever met, and we've never seen a shorter Life Line, not before or since. Jerry's Life Line was no more than an inch and a half long. If old-style theories that say a short Life Line equals a short life were true, Jerry should have shuffled off this mortal coil long, long ago. But Jerry's Life Line, short as it was, was also one of the *deepest* Life Lines we've ever seen. Truly, it looked almost as if it were carved into his palm.

Jerry is what we call a *Hot Chile Pepper*. Hot Chile Peppers have Life Lines that are quite deep, deep enough to stand out boldly, even if you look at them from a few feet away. A person with such a deeply graven Life Line is the proud possessor of a personality that retains its vitality, heat, and spice long into old age. *Attitude* is the important concept here. Individuals with deep Life Lines are not prepared to go quietly and meekly into their later years. No, their style rings with the kind of passion that Welsh poet Dylan Thomas expressed when he urged, "Do not go gentle into that good night"!

Hot Chile Peppers tend to approach confrontation without fear or favor, aiming to give as good as they get. But they are also wonderfully expressive friends, and you won't ever be in doubt about where you stand with them. Easy to anger, they are quick to forgive and prefer hugs to handshakes. Their commitment to life is physical as well as emotional, and they are always there for you when the chips are down. Have you ever run out of gas in the middle of the night? Or have you collapsed while giving a talk at a conference due to a bad shipment of shellfish? Your friend the Hot Chile Pepper will show up in his GMC C5500 tow truck to save you. Should you eat some bad oysters, he'll be there in the waiting room with the rest of your family until the doctors say you're on the path to recovery. At times their somewhat confrontational manner may be a trial to put up with, but when you find yourself in unusual circumstances you will absolutely bless your good fortune in having a Hot Chile Pepper for a friend.

## The Jazz on the Veranda Type

Some people have finer, more delicate Life Lines. These Life Lines speak of a sensibility, a way of aging, that's very different from the Hot Chile Pepper's Life Line. *Discernment* and *sophistication* are the key concepts here. Someone who possesses this kind of Life Line will age like fine wine, living life in savored sips and making sure to experience life deeply and intelligently. Like a fine meal that one remembers weeks, months, even years later, these folks more than anything else want to make sure that they maximize each experience—whether it's entertaining friends, putting on a surprise birthday party for their significant other, or taking classes in photography or French at the local community college.

We call this type of person the *Jazz on the Ve-*

*randa* type, and Claire is a good example of it. In her late seventies, she's all about family and friends, with a full schedule of socializing. She's known for her volunteerism in the community. While our friend Jerry (with the short Life Line) is like a very strong cup of coffee taken black, Claire is smooth and subtle, the kind of individual who affects everyone around her in low-key ways that have long-lasting effects. For example, Claire teaches classes in the art of quilting, after hours at the local community college. Her classes are always full. Her approach to the art form she has chosen is humorous and intellectual, and her enthusiasm for her craft is infectious. Claire, like all Jazz on the Veranda types, is Apollo to the typical Hot Chile Pepper's all-singing, all-dancing Dionysius. And her Life Line is as finely drawn as Chinese calligraphy.

## Action Heroes

Some people's Life Lines start out light and delicate and then become deep. We call these people *Action Heroes*. Action Heroes prefer jobs that involve lots of movement and the use of physical energy. A good example of the Action Hero is

Linda, who spent two years in law school before she came to the momentous decision to head off in a completely different direction. Almost overnight she dropped her bookish existence and went to work for the parks and recreation department in her local community. With her finely honed ability to communicate and her abundant physical energy, she now excels at working high-school kids through a confidence-building program. When we asked Linda what caused her sudden turnaround, the switch from a legal career of client meetings and filing briefs to a life of constant physical activity, she told us that, even though she enjoyed the study and intellectual work that went into studying law, she felt cut off from her true passion in life. One day, sitting in the stacks in the college library, she asked herself what she would do if she could do anything she wanted? The answer was simple. Now, she's playing out the answer that came from a place deep within her.

Linda's story is typical of Action Heroes. Like Clark Kent, Superman's alter ego, the action heros—before they truly find themselves—live quite ordinary lives. They pursue normal careers and have average successes. However, at some point, the Action Hero is likely to suddenly "get it." They will connect with a deeply felt sense of what they should, or need, to be doing in life. And they do it.

## Where Does the Life Line Fall on the Palm?

Always take note of where the Life Line falls on the palm. How far does it extend out into the central area of the palm? Some Life Lines swing out in a wide arc that reaches almost to the middle of the palm, and others make a close circle around the base of the thumb. And some fall somewhere in the middle. Each of these locations indicates a different approach to life and its experiences. Let's take a look.

### FAR TRAVELERS

Some people's Life Lines extend almost out to the middle of their palm—these people we call *Far Travelers*. Far Travelers have an approach to life that is expansive. Life to the Far Traveler is a journey; their bags are packed and their passports stamped. They are prepared to go anywhere. Some of the traveling that Far Travelers do is metaphorical rather than literal. To them, life is a voyage. Everything—waking up in the morning, heading to work, going to school, getting an education, even having a relationship—is a kind of traveling, a voyage with a beginning, a middle, and a final arrival at the destination.

Far Travelers are not bashful about introducing themselves to their fellow voyagers. Because of this characteristic, Far Travelers make friends easily and quickly. While some feel shy about introducing themselves to complete strangers or striking up conversations with people in settings like parties, airports, libraries, and cafeterias, this is not the case with Far Travelers. Their list of acquaintances is usually just this side of vast. Far Travelers are people people, and they are usually masters of the art of the schmooze. Connecting with others is their thing; they make good salespeople and human resource managers.

That said, Far Travelers' friendships are not

necessarily deep ones. Because of their expansive natures, they have room for lots of people and lots of conversations. At a party they will feel most comfortable playing the field and circulating continually. They will not necessarily take the time or give the energy to get to know any particular person or topic of conversation in depth.

Because they like the social whirl, these people become adept at the art of conversation. You'll recognize a Far Traveler because he'll usually be in a group talking comfortably and quickly and with more gusto than the others. Like expert pool players and experienced musicians, Far Travelers give their conversation a special wrinkle, a spice, that makes what they say just a little bit more memorable than the conversation of the people that surround them—and because of this, we remember what they say. The distinctive way Far Travelers speak can make them the target of the mimicry of their friends and loved ones. The Far Traveler's speech is that distinctive. They carry themselves in ways that other people not so gifted in these areas remember, even years later.

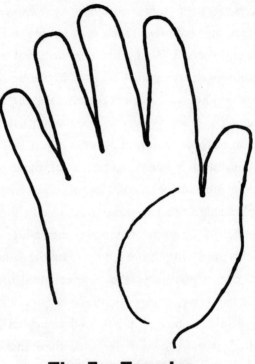

**The Far Traveler**

THERE'S NO PLACE LIKE HOME
If you see a Life Line that stays very close to the
base of the thumb, making a tight circle, that person is what we call a *No-Place-Like-Homer*, a dis-

tinctive breed! In some of the older palmistry traditions, an expansive, stretching Life Line (like
that of a Far Traveler) meant that the personality
was generous and outgoing, whereas those who
did *not* have this quality (like a No-Place-Like-
Homer) must be as stingy as Scrooge on a bad
day. Not so. We've found that people whose Life
Line tightly circles the thumb have a keen sense
of roots, of family, of friends. With these people
there is a dramatic sense of inside and outside;
they tend to be more concerned with maintaining, enjoying, and improving their sense of
home life than they are with getting to know
everything happening in the great world out
there. Although No-Place-Like-Homers may
journey far afield, racking up as many frequent-
flyer miles as their Far Traveler companions,
they will *always* have as their most important area
of emphasis that place they call home and the
small and important circle of loved ones who
compose it.

Although No-Place-Like-Homers can be good
schmoozers in their own right, this is not where
their hearts' desire lies. People with these Life

Lines are much more concerned with a truly fantastic Thanksgiving or Christmas celebration than with a masked ball at which the mayor might appear. They'll attend public occasions— no problem!—but they positively revel in loved-ones-only events. No-Place-Like-Homers will look for any excuse to turn each day into a celebration. They love birthdays, anniversaries, even christenings, but in a pinch they'll celebrate whatever comes to mind.

If you're reading the palm of someone who has a closely held Life Line, you can appear almost psychic by telling her that she very likely keeps a scrapbook of some kind, a book that she fills with pictures and memorabilia. Look also for journal keepers among people with Life Lines that hug the base of the thumb. For the No-Place-Like-Homer, keeping tangible reminders of her experiences is a necessity.

These people define themselves not by the number of friends they have but by the depth of their friendships. They would much rather have a single friend or partner whom they know well and share everything with, than a hundred glittering acquaintances.

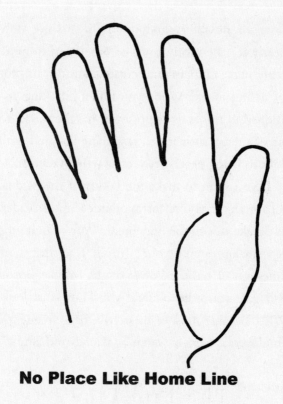

**No Place Like Home Line**

THE POWER OF THE MIDDLE

If you see a Life Line that steers a clear course midway between the Far Traveler and the No-Place-Like-Homer, that person is what we call the Power of the Middle. The Life Line placed in this position between the two extremes gives its possessor flexibility and the ability to not only clearly see the motivations of others but to more freely make choices (and create a custom fit!) for his desires in life. When you find a Life Line positioned in this way, its possessor has the power to act as a negotiator in many situations, often with skills to bring peace between warring factions.

If you want to make the Power of the Middle person think you're an apprentice mind reader, just make this simple statement: "You're quite the peacemaker, aren't you?" You'll find that nine times out of ten the Power of the Middle person will give you a how-could-you-know-that look. Why? Because most of them have been frequently employed as a go-between by friends and family.

# The Life Line's Beginning, Ending, and Meaning

### AMBITION

A Life Line beginning high up, directly under the first finger, indicates ambition. Remember, the role of the index finger is about the public self, about involvement in business relationships, so the linking of Life Line and index finger is a powerful combination.

## CREATIVITY

A Life Line ending on the percussive side of the hand shows Luna's pull—a creative tide exerts an influence on this life. Typically, this goes hand in hand with a deep desire for travel, as if travel somehow functions to unleash the creative.

## A MARK OF FORTUNE

A line that runs parallel to, and inside the curve of, the Life Line is a sister line. The sister lines are a mark of fortune; they indicate an element of protection in the area where they occur:

- If at the beginning of the Life Line, there's protection in the early life.
- If at the end of the Life Line, there's protection in the later life.

In real-life terms, this means protection during otherwise difficult events—perhaps mitigating a health event or stress at work. We call this the *Guardian Angel* line.

## A BREAK

A break in the Life Line indicates a remarkable life change. In the older books on palmistry, this is sometimes called the "gap of emigration." Marty has a break in his Life Line. We asked him if he had experienced a serious life change. Marty said, yes, he'd experienced a dramatic change: He had a very serious eye problem. In fact, he was going blind. On the eve of going in for a very dangerous eye surgery, Marty called his broker and directed him to take all his money out of the stock market. His stockbroker did as Marty requested, and while Marty was recovering from his eye surgery, the market did one of its nose dives. His eye surgery a success and his money intact, Marty had a profound revelation about the shortness and sweetness of life. He now spends his time hiking all the national parks—a dramatic departure from his former lifestyle.

Yes, a break in the Life Line indicates a complete change of life state.

# Does the Life
# Line Change?

Do the lines on the palm change? This is a question we get asked frequently. And the answer is yes. The Life Line—and, to some extent, the other major lines in the hand—does change. Like everything else that is human, our personalities are transformed as we experience life, and our hands reflect those changes.

# The Heart Line

The Heart Line is the topmost of the major lines of the palm, running just under the fingers, from the little finger side of the hand, typically ending somewhere below the middle or ring fingers (the Saturn or Jupiter fingers). Before a baby is born, the Heart Line is the first line that forms in utero. It forms long before the muscles develop, and because of this, palm readers, both old-style and *Palms Up!*–types, have always maintained that the Heart Line clearly reflects something deep, something basic, something innate about our nature that we bring into the world when we are born. This line is all about how we relate to others, to ourselves, and to our world. Of course, the Heart Line is also about romance and partners, about love and sex.

Most people who come to us to have their palms read are interested, specifically, in taking a look at what their palms have to say about romance. They are especially interested in hearing if the lines on their palm can give them any idea when they will meet Mr. or Ms. Right. And although palm reading by itself can't give you much of an idea about the when (that's more natural to divinatory practices like numerology and astrology) it can give you glimpses into ways to figure out if any particular individual is likely to work out for you in the romance department.

The Heart Line gives us a global picture of our emotional life: our attitudes to everything, our relationships with everyone we interact with—it's all captured in the Heart Line. The first thing to look for when trying to get a picture of the Heart Line is where it begins and where it ends.

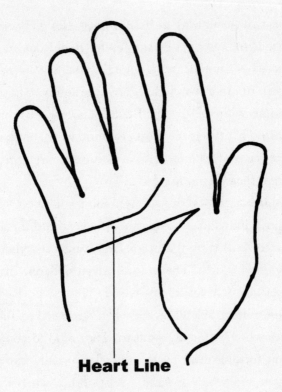

**Heart Line**

# Ending Between
# Your Index and
# Middle Fingers

Perhaps the most common line is one that starts beneath the baby finger and then curves across the palm and up, to end slightly below and between the Jupiter and Saturn fingers. This is ideal in that it reflects a balance between personal needs (represented by the Jupiter finger) and the needs of another (represented by the Saturn finger). In other words, this shows the ability to be at home with the give and take of a real relationship. That this is the most common configuration we see underscores that we as humans are wired for a shared emotional life.

If you possess this configuration, you're one of those individuals who can manage the difficult act of balancing the needs (and wants) of others with your own. This is a nontrivial skill, one that can take you far in this world. Those who have this trait are able to say no when they need to, and yes when they truly want to. They tend to commit to long-term relationships but usually know how and when to leave a relationship when it's not going anywhere.

## Ending Under Your Index Finger

If your Heart Line ends under the index finger, this means that although you love deeply, there's a part of yourself that you keep *for* yourself, a kind of secret garden where to be at your best emotionally and socially, you need (almost require) a certain amount of down time. We like to say that people with Heart Lines that end under the index finger have a place that is password-protected, a place that even those very close to them may never know about. It can take years for these folks to reveal certain aspects of their personality, even to their loved ones.

This does not mean that someone with this characteristic is in any way moody or introverted. In fact, Heart Lines reaching up to end under the Jupiter finger (the first finger) show personalities that are naturally expressive, ones that like to hear and see audible and visible signs of the affection that others feel—and may even have just a wee bit of a tendency toward jealousy, of expecting others to show the same degree of expressiveness in matters of love as they do, which not everyone is capable of.

## Ending Under Your Middle Finger

If your Heart Line ends under your middle finger then you give, give, give to the people you love—and then you give some more. You give because it makes you happy. Much of your happiness is a result of the emotions and the growth that you create and give to other people. You take friendship seriously. When (or if ) you have children, you will love-bomb them with great frequency.

With that said, those who have a Heart Line that ends under the middle finger have a tendency (at times) to overlook themselves and their own deepest needs. Because they are so attuned to the needs of others, they can sometimes find themselves in situations in which they are baffled by the simple fact that they must put themselves first, to make a necessary decision that puts their own needs before the needs of others. This can be very difficult for them to do.

One of the most common things that we have noticed about people with this characteristic is that they seem to attract what we can only describe as *hitchhikers*. Because of their warmth, generosity, and concern for others, these people attract others who are in crisis. Those with Heart Lines that end underneath the middle finger are always there for other people, and they can make a career of fielding the crisis calls of loved ones and friends. The trouble is that what begins as a phone call can often turn into more. They can find themselves pulled into the emotional disorder of other people's lives. We find ourselves urging such people to make decisions that, although they already know they *must* make, they just can't bring themselves to make.

### *Palms Up!* Prescription

Those with Heart Lines ending under the middle finger are prone to attracting hitchhikers. Learn to say no. Although your shoulders are broad and strong, it won't hurt for other people to fend for themselves from time to time. It will help them grow.

The Heart Line ending under the middle finger sometimes will also indicate a person with a more reserved personality, someone who may have a harder time expressing emotion than others. These people may even (very paradoxically for someone so community oriented) project a persona that seems to not care very deeply for those around them. This is actually not the case. These individuals are often searchers, people whose main motivation is to feel and understand love; they just do not feel as comfortable expressing their emotions as others do. These people will frequently surprise you by displaying a depth of emotion and affection for others you did not think they possessed.

## Short Heart Lines

Occasionally you'll read the Heart Line of someone who has a very short line—one that ends well shy of the middle finger. Oddly enough, a short Heart Line is an indicator of a happy and straightforward emotional life. With the people who possess such a line, you will find no hidden agendas or subterranean needs. These folks are who and what they seem in their relationships—a fortunate few. While the rest of the world complicate their lives, juggling needs and wants like the Flying Karamazov Brothers juggling chainsaws with a semidemented look, those with short Heart Lines are easy and fun people to be with.

# Heart Lines That End in a Fork

Some Heart Lines end in a fork, or even multiple forks. The branching at the end of the line shows a very rich emotional life and abundant emotional energy. This often goes along with an artistic personality, especially when it's combined with a Head Line that curves down toward the Mount of Luna, or a long palm, or long fingers— other signs of a creative nature. The reader can learn valuable information from these forks by determining how many forks there are and whether they run toward the index finger or the middle finger.

## COUNTING THE FORKS

The rule for counting the forks is simple: the more lines you find, the more the person will be influenced in the direction that the forks point toward. We've seen as many as five lines (which is quite a number!) at the end of the Heart Line. Each of these faint lines adds emphasis to the characteristic being displayed. Sometimes these lines will be very fine and hard to see under normal room light. We each carry a magnifying glass to see the finer, more intimate details that can tell a lot about someone.

## WHICH DIRECTION DO THE FORKS HEAD?

If your forks are heading off toward your index finger, then something deep within you is looking for more (sometimes *much* more) in the way of your public life. This can indicate personal ambitions that you may never have shared with anyone else, even those closest to you. Have you always wanted to become a writer? Do you love mysteries and have wondered in your heart of hearts if you had it in you to become a Patricia Cornwell or the next Agatha Christie? If your forks travel toward your index finger, it's probably also an indication that you're yearning for private space and time. As a reader you will see this feature often, especially on strong, ambitious women with schedules that would intimidate a Donald Trump. Here, the fork is an indication of a need to emphasize the world that belongs to the individual over the needs of the community.

*Palms Up!* **Prescription**

If you find that you have a fork traveling toward your index finger, we recommend that you take a day off. Don't tell anyone, but go and do something you've always wanted to do just for yourself: see a movie, visit an art museum, go shopping, take a ferry ride, see a tourist site in the place where you live that you've never taken the time to visit. Yes, this will feel just a *little* strange, but that will be part of the fun, part of what makes it interesting. Experience some time by yourself— for yourself.

If your fork travels toward your middle finger, it indicates you are looking for a greater and stronger connection to friends, family, and/or community. We've noticed that very independent people with high public profiles show this trait often. These are individuals who spend the bulk of their time making their very public way in the world. They often have specific goals and make deep sacrifices to reach them. Their eyes are on the prize. And yet, these forks remind us, there is something missing. A fork, or a number of forks, can be an indication that you need to remember the ties that bind you to your friends, family, and community of which you are an important part. Often you need to relax for a moment, take a broader view, and connect with your sense of what we call your *immediate history*. Immediate history can mean the stories of your family (mother, father, great-great-grandmothers and grand-fathers), the tale of the small town you grew up in, or the story of the city or town you've come to live in.

The keyword for a fork that runs toward the middle finger is *reconnect*. It is advice to you, straight from the lines on your palm.

### *Palms Up!* Prescription

If you have a fork that runs toward your middle finger, try the following recommendations: (1) Call a relative that you haven't spoken to in years. Ask him about some bit of family history you've always wanted to catch up on. You'll be amazed at how willing blood ties are to give you their view on stories you *thought* you knew well. (2) Volunteer; communities are created from the shared experiences of strangers. Thinking about volunteering is much different from actually doing it. Once you've gotten together with a group of people to create an event or make yourself useful to a larger group of people, you will get benefits you've never imagined.

Forks that head in *both* directions at the same time indicate you're in the presence of an individual who is reaching for two (very different) things at once. She wants to live a quiet meditative life while also appearing before stadiums full of cheering adoring fans. We see this most often on people who are superachievers, the kind of person who is destined to make her mark in the world. These people usually desire a close family life and a tight-knit circle of friends to whom they are available 24/7—whatever the weather, whatever the circumstances. They desire an almost monastic sense of peace, order, and tranquility, a life in which they can contemplate and discover who, in fact, they really and truly are. They want to find out what they are capable of and are focused on a single burning goal. Along with this desire comes the wish to call the shots, make the decisions. They would like the ability to plan (by themselves) and execute the desires that well up from some deep personal spot inside of their souls.

### *Palms Up!* Prescription

If you have forks that run simultaneously toward both the index finger and the middle finger, we recommend you give yourself time, time to lighten up and relax. Start the barbecue, invite friends over, chill the wine. Although your ambition to have it all and be it all is noble—and we love you for it—the likelihood that you will achieve this unlikely dream is just that, unlikely. But we wish you well, and we'll be there for you when you fall short of the perfection you seek.

FORKS HAVE MAGNETIC
PERSONALITIES

Often people with the branching Heart Line are perceived as very attractive. But these people also have their ups and downs emotionally; life can be a real roller-coaster ride. What tends to make the difference for most people we've seen is the quality of their primary relationships. Grounded in a secure, supportive relationship, people with branched Heart Lines can be secure and happy, although they will always have some aspects of their emotional life that they don't share. With that emotional side of herself grounded in a good relationship, the personality with a branched Heart Line can quite easily overcome the up-and-down emotions she feels and excel in creative tasks.

# The Shape of the Heart Line

A Heart Line that proceeds straight and level across the palm can sometimes indicate a person who would rather not show their affection in public. If you'd like to tease a person with a straight Heart Line, you can pull an extremely naughty prank by mauling him in public. Although extremely responsive in private, he will positively squirm when you make amorous advances in the midst of crowds. Try it, and see if we aren't calling it like it is. These straight-across-the-palm Heart Line folks typically need more psychic space within a relationship and tend to carry a torch for loves lost.

On the other hand, those with Heart Lines that curve up are extremely comfortable with expressing their innermost feelings in public settings. At the beach or the mall, they're the ones who demand hugs (and more) as signs of affection.

Some people have Heart Lines that go in two directions. Angie is a good example. Her Heart Line is long and straight across most of her palm, and then, near the end, it suddenly splits and curves sharply upward. If you're on her favored list, you get hugs from Angie. She brims with energy and enthusiasm. In relationships, she gives 110 percent. The levelness of her Heart Line gives her a quality that makes her intense and loyal, protective and supportive. The (mostly) straightforwardness of her Heart Line makes her the perfect person to serve as someone's assistant and right-hand person; a low-profile pinch hitter with a flair for doing the legwork. The sharp upward turn at the end of her Heart Line gives her the ability to turn up the heat and charm whenever she feels so inclined.

## Branching

Branches curving down from the Heart Line show disappointments, not just in personal relationships, but in our emotional life in general; we've never seen a hand without a few of these. Branches curving up from the Heart Line indicate good fortune, not just in personal relationships, but also in collaborative work and personal efforts.

## The Subject Is Sex

As a *Palms Up!* palm reader, sooner or later, you'll find that when you get to the Heart Line a high percentage of people whose palms you read will want to talk about the *S*-word: sex. It's natural.

By the time we talk about the Heart Line, we will have talked about finger length, the Mighty Thumb, Free Agents and Team Players, and the Life Line. The mysteries of the Heart Line, then, are left until you've had a chance to get comfortable with the person whose hand you're reading.

Why? A number of reasons, actually. First of all, as a *Palms Up!* palm reader you will find yourself invited into intimate spaces by complete strangers (by talking with them about the way they handle decisions, how they relate to other people), and it will take at least some time for them to get comfortable with you. Very natural. It is also natural for them to be just a bit skeptical and cautious about the art of palm reading. But by the time you've looked at (and laughed about) features like their thumbs, telling them whether they make decisions quickly in the best Leaper fashion or slowly and methodically as a true and cautious Looker, they will have discarded their skepticism and be wondering just exactly how deeply you might be able to see into their most secret selves.

Count on it. Many of those whose palms you read will also be curious about taking that one further step and discussing the most intimate subject of all: sex. And by looking at their Heart Lines, you'll be able to talk to them about just that subject. Read on and we'll tell you how.

## PLEASERS AND PLEASE ME'S

Where the Heart Line ends is extremely important in matters of sex. Old-school palm readers have always touted the idea that the "best" place for the Heart Line to end is directly between the index and middle fingers. It indicates that the person whose palm you're reading is adept at juggling the often competing needs of others (represented by the middle finger, the finger of community) and herself (signified by the index finger, the finger of the self).

We agree that this is true. Especially in family and romantic relationships.

But this is only half of the story, just as love is only half of the story when it comes to matters of the heart. Sex is the other half of the story. In sex there really is no *best* place, no perfect ideal that every human being must live up to. In matters of pleasure, what counts is what *is*—the reality of personal likes and desires and the ways each person's own pleasure principle interacts with those she chooses to be intimate with. Either something gives you pleasure, or it doesn't. The fact that it *should* give you pleasure, when it doesn't, is of little help.

What does help is self-knowledge, knowing about what does and does not please you in the most intimate matters. So, are you a Pleaser or a Please Me?

If your Heart Line ends under your middle finger, you're a Pleaser in intimate matters. The pleasure of your partner is the one element indispensable to you in matters of sex. Without his turn-on, you will be unsatisfied. In fact for the Pleaser, true intimacy requires having an effect on a partner, an effect that is unquestionable, obvious, even blatant.

For a Pleaser, a relationship depends heavily (and ultimately) on the ability to give pleasure. When the ability to give pleasure is consistently present in a relationship, then whatever hardships come along—financial stresses, employment hassles—the Pleaser will be able to weather them, staying upbeat and productive. Without this one key element, any relationship will be, not impossible, but a struggle.

This is more, much more, than a simple case of needing to be needed. Pleasers can be and, in fact, usually are very confident in matters of the heart and extremely comfortable with their own sexuality and matters of intimacy. They do not generally need constant strokes to be confident of their worth in a relationship. But, in matters of sex, they will achieve satisfaction *only* when they play an important part in their partner's achieving it.

If your Heart Line ends under your index finger, you're a Please Me. Sex for you is about the inner experience. The feelings, the responses, the desires you have are centered around your individual experience, your individual experiments with intimacy.

This is *not* about selfishness or self-centeredness. Please Me's are neither of these things. They are warm and frequently generous people, especially in matters of the bedroom. They not only get the nod for plays well with others, but are especially inclusive when it comes to the needs of their partners.

Their viewpoint is very different from most Pleasers. While the Pleaser will derive satisfaction from the pleasure of his partner, the Please Me will assume that his experience is the same as his partner's. As a partner, he will work with (appropriate) passion to build his own experience with creativity and focus.

## Intimate Area Ahead, Tread Softly

A word of warning: When talking to people about sensitive areas, use caution. Always remember that when you show someone these aspects of the palm, you should take the *Palms Up!* approach: A modern, twenty-first-century way of speaking about the various aspects of their Heart Line. Remember that a single aspect or line is only that: a single, solitary feature, one that may be modified a little bit (or a lot) by other features of the hand. Use discretion. As a palm reader your goal is to entertain, so never be dogmatic. You'll have more fun that way.

# The Head Line

By now the lines on your palm should be getting much more familiar to you. You know the terrain better. Looking down at the palm of your dominant hand (the one you sign your product endorsements with!), very close to the start of your Life Line, you'll see another line that, instead of circling the base of the thumb, heads out across the palm in a more or less straight line. This is your Head Line.

The Head Line runs across the middle of your palm, more or less. It runs below the Heart Line, unless you are one of those rare people with only one line running across the palm, in which case we will talk later, because you are special. But for the rest of us, the Head Line runs across the palm below the Heart Line. It may run straight across the palm, from between the thumb and forefinger to the percussive side of the hand, or it may curve downward toward the wrist. As with all the lines, the intensity of the line equates to a person's engagement in the activity the line represents: A deep clear Head Line shows an active intelligence.

Since the Head Line is located between the Life Line and the Heart Line, we like to think of it as the go-between, a much needed buffer between our emotions and our vitality.

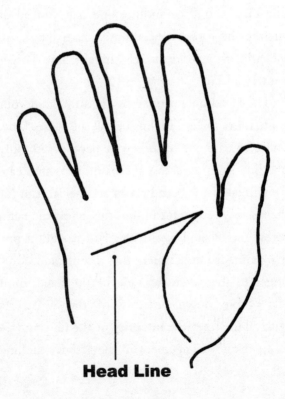

**Head Line**

# Level Head Lines

A level Head Line runs across the palm in a straight line, starting from under the index finger and heading over toward the very edge of the hand, under the baby finger.

Are you extremely practical? Do you prefer life to be a straightforward affair? Do complications piling up tend to rattle your cage and make you feel like climbing the wall? Do you have a knack for cutting to the chase, an ability to see the shortest distance between two points? All right, enough with the quiz. If you have a Head Line that proceeds directly across the palm with nary a dip or turn, you feel an instinctive aversion to the type of person who is always beating around the bush, the kind of person who seems allergic to getting to the point. What *you* say, you *do*.

As a *Palms Up!* palm reader, we call you a *True Seer*.

No, you can't see off into the near or distant future like a psychic or a fortune teller. What you *do* have is the ability to see what's right in front of you on the plate. The True Seer calls them as she sees them.

As a True Seer, you're a joy to work with and for, because (unlike many other folks) you actually do the things that you commit to. Your friends count on you to act as a judge at times, because you are able to see through a mass of details and conflicting accounts to get at that kernel of truth that, once addressed, makes even the most complicated situation come out right, and come out fair. You have a low tolerance for aggravation at times, especially when you find yourself involved in a project which someone else is supervising. Being able to see a clearer, simpler way of getting things done can make for an annoying experience. It is a basic part of your nature to be on time, unlike some of your friends. When you borrow a book, it doesn't become part of your collection, and it certainly won't be passed on down the line to another reader. You'll return it. Count on it.

Of course this means that this world can put you in a state of advanced exasperation. But you are able to handle even these situations with a certain evenness, a certain level-headedness that is the envy of your less-solid, less-stable companions.

In the palm reading of the past, a person with a level Head Line was characterized as someone with a completely unimaginative way of dealing with the world. Don't make the same mistake! The level Head Line of the True Seer does *not* mean unimaginative; we have found it indicates a person with the kind of imagination that is energetic, direct, and sets out on her mission *without* waiting for inspiration before making her first move. Because their approach to life is so direct, so straight ahead, True Seers seem very rooted to others. They tend to think matters through, consider their options, and come to a personal take. And once they've done that, they let the matter rest.

This letting-the-matter-rest behavior is *so* different from the way most people conduct their mental lives that it makes people with level Head Lines stand out. While others seem to be coming to their "final" revelation on this, that, or the other topic on an almost daily basis, True Seers have made their judgment calls long ago and are sticking to them. True Seers have a tendency to take the long view on many matters. They have a love of that which lasts, and they don't ride the trends. This does not mean they're deaf to the world of style. Far from it. True Seers can often be among the most observant and knowledgeable decoders of trends happening in the world of fashion or the arts. It's often been said that the best analysts come from the ranks of those who don't play a particular game or sport themselves. In this case it's true.

## The La Mancha Head Line

Unlike the level True Seers, the *La Mancha* Head Line curves—boy, does it curve! Those who have this type of Head Line seek to dream the impossible dream. (Hence our nickname for this line!) When you see this type of Head Line, note how radical the curve is. Does the Head Line describe a gradual curve, one that you'd have no trouble negotiating on a set of rollerblades? Or does it look like you'd need Everest-level climbing gear, pitons, and hundreds of feet of nylon rope to rappel down its steep sides? We've seen both the gradual and the radically curved—everything from the slightly sloping to Head Lines that look very much like they are taking diving lessons from their big sister the Life Line.

## DIVING TOWARD LUNA

If you follow the slope of the dramatically diving La Mancha line, you'll get a view of what it's diving toward—a place on the palm called the Mount of Luna. The Mount of Luna is on the side of the palm farthest away from the thumb. To find it, hold your palm up like you're going to deliver a stunning karate chop—the side of the palm that you're delivering the blow with is called the percussion side. The place right around the corner, on the surface of the palm, is the Mount of Luna. In palmistry, the moon speaks for the symbolic, the imaginative, the mysterious. If the True Seers like their world straightforward, direct, explainable, and on time, La Manchas are reaching for . . . well, other things.

La Manchas are born romantics (the more slope, the more romanticism), they are always looking for that mysterious something that they'll only *truly* know when they find it. They're a bit moonstruck, and they love to be in love. In fact, they *need* to be in love. Nothing depresses them more than the idea that the life stretching before them is a flat plain unrelieved by high mountains and deep valleys. This need for romance can drive them in some fairly dramatic directions.

La Manchas are natural-born enthusiasts, cheerleaders. They take a positive attitude toward life and enjoy doing everything they possibly can with verve and gusto. Some may accuse them of not living in the real world and to some extent, this is true; La Manchas live in the world they *want* to see come into existence, a world that they will work (sometimes *very* hard) to create. La Manchas are very future-oriented, and it's hard to get them down to terra firma.

Being so future-oriented makes many La Manchas skillful and effective as counselors, with a knack for talking people out of bad moods, bad decisions, and thinking patterns. It's actually difficult to get into a truly full funk around a La Mancha because he possesses what amounts to a kind of four-wheel drive of the intellectual and emotional life. Of course some people can manage their own personal emotional lives and certainly don't need the help that the dedicated La Mancha can give them. Tough.

Remember, we told you that La Manchas are dedicated? They *will* cheer you up, with an insistence that some will resist with gritted teeth. When a La Mancha is devotedly attempting to give you an overdose of his own version of *Chicken Soup for the Soul,* you can only pray that you have the strength to endure his maddeningly insistent encouragement.

If you go into the house or apartment of a La Mancha, look on the walls. La Manchas prefer images that are a bit mysterious and usually deeply symbolic, the kind of pictures that remind us of images from dreams. Another favorite decoration strategy of the La Mancha is to make a place that is very altar-like, sometimes in the bedroom or in the living room. La Manchas like to have a place, a personal space, if you will, that reflects their deepest intuitions and sense of the mysterious in their lives. For some this means having a place where objects are arranged in an artful way, a way that telegraphs to the onlooker that something deeply personal, even private, is going on in an intimate space created in the living environment. Sometimes these places reflect a deep wit, a sense of humor, usually irreverent.

Sometimes this area is not an altar-like arrangement but a scrapbook—a scrapbook that is fully articulated. Fully articulated? In the hands of someone with a dramatically dipping Head Line, the scrapbook will become an art object. Although the scrapbook may have started as a mere container of photographs and a few items of memorabilia, it evolves into something that goes far beyond that, taking the scrapbook that we associate with the family photo album into another dimension entirely.

At its base, the desire of the La Manchas with their curving Head Lines is for the deeply per-sonalized space, and the scrapbook fulfills their need to express the romance, drama, and—yes—spirituality that they feel is a basic part of life in some physically substantial form, a form that can both be seen *and* felt. It is also a part of their principled stand on the meaning of life. They seem to be saying, *here* is the meaning of life, the deep meaning that lies beneath the surface; come share it with me.

La Manchas are very sensitive and tuned to their environment. Because they crave a deep sense of the romantic in their lives, they want a home that is more, much more, than simply four walls, some windows, a yard, a cat, and a place to park the generic car with four wheels and a steering wheel. They want the place they live and spend their time in to reflect their sensibilities and viewpoint. When you go into the house of a La Mancha, look for *Architectural Digest* and *Sunset* magazines. These individuals will also tend to have projects on the back burner, sometimes as many as half a dozen, because—we can't emphasize this enough—they are deeply into *personalizing* their environment.

## Breaks in the Head Line

Sometimes you'll see a break in a person's Head Line. The old-school interpretation for this was that it represents a period of time when the person isn't thinking, perhaps due to illness or injury. But as you read the palms of your closest friends, you'll see that this classic explanation doesn't always work. You're likely instead to find that breaks in the Head Line represent drastic changes in the way a person thinks about his life. Here's an example: At a recent event, we met a young man, Saul, who had a significant break in his Head Line. Talking to him revealed no periods of unconsciousness or illness in his past. Instead, Saul had spent a period of time in a teaching career. He was fully engaged in and enjoyed his work, and he was successful. But in a period of six months, he had given up his teaching job and embarked on a career as a musician and writer. It was a total about-face in his beliefs about himself and how he thought about his life, which was shown by the break in an otherwise strong Head Line.

# A Head Line That Starts Out Connected to the Life Line

The Head Line begins between the thumb and the forefinger, but it may begin either as a single strand connected to the Life Line, or it may start out as a distinctly separate line. When the Head Line and the Life Line start connected, as one line, they signify an intelligence that develops as part of a family unit—with shared values, with the community as an ideal. Most people don't grow up in a perfect, communal existence, so when we see the joined Head and Life Lines, we also typically see chaining or islands, indicating early tension and strife, with the gradual separation indicating a personality that developed individual awareness, individual thought, and matured into an idiosyncratic, individuated self. People with these conjoined lines never really lose that sense of the importance of the family or community connection. They'll take with them throughout life a strong sense of the need of a shared bond and a longing for it. They miss it when it's absent from their lives; they'll work hard to create it.

## A Head Line That Starts Out on Its Own

Those with distinctly separate Head and Life Lines have never been led by the siren song of belonging. They don't feel a particularly keen need for the validation of others. And the idea that they have a connection with someone else because of a blood tie seems extremely theoretical. In considering a relationship with a person with a separated Head and Life Line, it is a good idea to consider how much of a freethinker you can handle. These separated Head and Life Line individuals will not be afraid to break the rules. They like thinking for (and by) themselves. Always have; always will. After all, it's the only way they truly know.

## Chains and Islands

Chains are looping or braid-like formations on the lines. Islands are loops, little squashed circles that stand by themselves. In both cases, they indicate turbulence.

In the case of those with distinctly separate Head and Life Lines, this turbulence is likely to be caused by the way the world deals with individualists, thinkers who spend much of their time seriously questioning everything.

## Ambition and the Head Line

You'll occasionally see the Head Line starting high up near the base of the Jupiter finger (the index finger). This shows ambition for success in a public arena. Quite often you find this line on the individual who believes in the power of the human mind to better one's life. This is the person who attends night classes, frequents book discussion clubs, is actively investing in herself, and constantly upgrading her brain skills.

## The Space Between

Look at the space between the Head and Heart Lines. It may be a perfectly even space, the lines paralleling each other evenly and precisely, or the space between these two lines may be narrow in the center, wider at either end.

If the space is an even width, it's the sign of a stable character; these people have an even temperament, at least, compared to the rest of humanity. Those with an even space between the Head and Heart Line are sometimes easier to be with—they are who they say they are, who they think they are. What you see is what you get.

If the space between the two lines is irregularly shaped, narrower in the middle than at either end, for example, it indicates a person who can oscillate over the years between supreme self-confidence and constant self-questioning. These people are constantly finding out just who they are, at times on an almost daily basis. They make lively and often inspiring companions who rouse in others a sense of the scope of life's journey.

## The Writer's Fork

Let's look at the ending of the Head Line: Does it branch? This is the writer's fork.

The writer's fork indicates the presence of the kind of mind that can develop scenarios, understand deep motivation, and create believable characters. It indicates the ability to communicate clearly. Obviously, these same skills are vital to people other than writers. Need to create a marketing plan, author a proposal, write a press release, or come up with an article for a Web site? Call out for someone with a writer's fork. It can be handy to have a writer's fork.

The writer's fork can appear on either the practical or the imaginative Head Line—the difference is the way people use the talents signified by the writer's fork.

At a summer event, Sheila met a young lady in jeans and a cashmere jacket with her mother in tow. The two were leaving on a cruise ship for Alaska the next morning. At the end of the younger woman's Head Line was one of the most distinctive (and deepest) writer's forks Sheila had ever seen. Sheila knew that the writer's fork is an indication of the kind of individual who can always see any situation from both sides. Sheila amazed the young woman by asking if she always saw the world from two sides.

"How do you know that?" she asked in wonderment.

Her mother simply shook her head, laughing. Sheila had scored a direct hit on her daughter using *Palms Up!* palmistry. It turned out the young woman was a musician's agent. She made a good living through her ability to simultaneously see both her artists' and an event promoter's point of view.

## Going Up?

An unusual ending to the Head Line is a sharp turn upwards at the end of the line, indicating an innate need for material success. These people may strike others as overly materialistic, but in fact they are expressing a real need for material acquisition—a basic (even primal) need. For people who have this feature, ignoring the desire is not an option. We once read the palms of a mother and daughter. They were both confident women who clearly liked each other. The mother's hands confirmed her sense of style, and her highly individual personality; her hands also showed that she could be a stern taskmaster when occasion demanded. The daughter had the upturned line at the end of the Head Line. When we told them what this upward turn meant, the mother turned to her daughter and said, "The white house with the pillars, remember?"

Apparently, when she was just a baby, the

daughter's earliest expressed desire had been to live in a big white house with pillars—an expression of her need for material success and the possessions that go along with success. By their reaction, we could tell that this had been a source of tension, perhaps a basic misunderstanding between them in the past. The mother and daughter pair nodded at each other, smiling. As they walked away laughing, we felt the reading had helped them understand (and accept) each other just a little bit better.

# A Rare Line

There is a rare line that unites the Head Line and the Heart Line into one line that crosses the palm below the fingers. Old-style palmists have been known to mutter darkly that the person who possesses such a line needs a quick check of his DNA to determine if he is quite human; they have dubbed this line the *simian line*. The logic of old-school readers of palms must have gone something like this: Without the Head Line and the Heart Line, we must be looking at a kind of prehuman line, a kind of throwback. Like the "murderer's" thumb, this feature is one of the most misunderstood in all of palmistry. We have read countless thousands of palms and encountered the combined Heart and Head Line perhaps only a dozen times. However, the people we find with this line are strikingly consistent. They are intense and have an almost religious sense of mission in life.

Those who have the combined line are similar to those who possess a Fate Line (more about this soon). They come into life equipped (most at a fairly early age) with a prominent and durable sense of purpose. Because they possess this, they often seem calmer and less concerned about matters like career and romance than others. But the people with this quality are also undeniably intense and appear driven to those around them, especially to their co-workers.

A good example is Jody, an executive with an advertising firm. Jody is the kind of employee who seems to attract awards: employee of the week, month, year; highest-grossing salesperson, and so on. Now, Jody is wonderfully charming and vital and obviously the kind of boss that

everyone dreams of—she has the ability to inspire, and she works long, hard hours when a project's delivery date is coming around. But she is
intense. When Mark said, "Jody, you are a very,
very intense woman," her co-workers burst out
laughing. "You better believe it," said one of her
partners.

The joined Head and Heart Lines indicate
someone who has high expectations for herself.
Why? A person with this configuration tends to
demand of herself an absolute congruence between her thoughts (the Head Line) and her feelings (the Heart Line), which means that she puts
her all into every activity she undertakes.

**A Rare Line**

# The Fate Line

As we've stated, the Fate Line is a misunderstood line. It has been called the line of destiny. It's also sometimes called the Saturn line, because it rises up from the bottom of the palm and heads toward the middle finger (the Saturn finger). This line—familiar (as a concept) to so many—is actually unusual; believe it or not, many people don't have one. Now, before we continue, let us be perfectly clear: Having no Fate Line doesn't mean you don't have a fate; this is old-fashioned thinking. In general, when modern palmists find a Fate

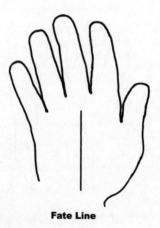

**Fate Line**

Line on someone's palm, they expect the person to have a special area of his life that he focuses on with drive and ambition, regardless of what he does for a living.

The absence of a Fate Line simply means that the person picks and chooses his life's path with a little more freedom than those who possess the line.

## Where the Fate Line Starts

• The Fate Line that starts close to the wrist shows an early awareness of destiny.

• A Fate Line starting on or inside the Life Line indicates a person following a path that keeps close to the family in some way; either following in a parent's footsteps, or working in an arena inspired or somehow associated with family interests.

• A Fate Line starting outside the Life Line reflects an independent beginning, and independent thinking; this is someone who will navigate according to her own stars.

• A Fate Line starting on the Mount of Luna, the area on the surface of the palm right next to the edge of the hand, signifies a need for creative work. This person must be involved in creative work and must follow that need or pay a huge price in dissatisfaction. It's typical for people with this kind of Fate Line to change jobs frequently, making leaps into different fields to further explore the creative life. When you see someone with this line who's stayed with the same work for a significant length of time, it's either because the work offers an endless learning curve for creative energy or external circumstances have blocked him from exercising his ability to choose his path. When that happens—and we've seen this with people who have been constrained by financial problems or family responsibilities—the individual generally has developed a major creative outlet that he pursues in his free time.

• A Fate Line that starts higher on the palm indicates someone who develops a focus later in life.

# Where the Fate Line Ends

Where the Fate Line ends is just as revealing as where it begins. We often see a strong Fate Line that stops at the Heart Line, indicating perhaps a conventional retirement; these are the folks who have worked hard to develop their careers, but then choose to leave the rat race behind and reap the rewards of all that hard work with a lifestyle that doesn't require the major commitment of a new, second career. But there are those who pursue their chosen work long after a conventional retirement age, and that shows in a Fate Line that reaches past the Heart Line to the base of the fingers.

- A Fate Line that ends under the index finger shows a leaning toward a public career: politics, perhaps, or law.
- A Fate Line that ends under the middle finger (the Saturn finger) is far more common, reflecting these folks' typical sense of the work they do—and get paid for—as something that they owe to an external

power, a duty they owe to their employers, or perhaps to their families.

• The Fate Line that ends below the ring finger is unusual. This indicates that the work done by the person will be creative, artistic.

• If the Fate Line ends under the baby finger, you are headed toward professions where communication is the focus. Television, film, work as a writer or actor—any of these could be in your future.

## Parallel Fate Lines

We frequently see a particular pattern in women's hands: A Fate Line that splits and forms parallel lines at or below the Head Line. This parallel Fate Line reflects the time during which women are equally committed to developing both career and family. The double line is common in women, but it occasionally appears in men, too. It may indicate the same priorities—career and family— but it sometimes simply reflects someone with more than one deep commitment or interest. The most unusual Fate Line we've ever seen, for several reasons, was a triple line that became a double line in later life. This unusual woman is a very successful therapist, a single mother, and a teacher—completely dedicated in each of her roles.

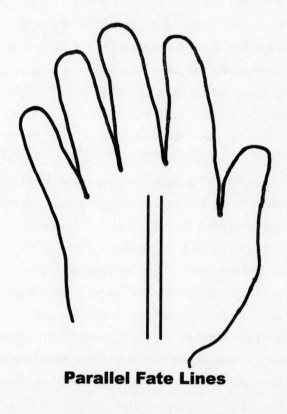

**Parallel Fate Lines**

# Relationship Lines: Children and Relationships

On the side of the hand, just beneath the place where the baby finger begins, you'll find the relationship lines. In old-school books on palmistry, the horizontal lines are called relationship lines, and the vertical lines are designated "children lines." Old-style palm readers would interpret the horizontal relationship lines as and indication of the number of marriages a person was likely to have. The vertical lines crossing these relationship lines would tell the palm reader how many children you would have. It was just this simple: if you had three vertical lines in this area, you would have three children. The twenty-first-century *Palms Up!* palm reader, knows that, like the short Life Line indicating a short, sweet life, this just isn't the case. Time and technology have simply changed the meaning and import of these lines completely. Today, we say that these lines speak of relationships. The deeper the line, the deeper and more central the relationship is. We also say that these lines do not necessarily signify marriage or offspring. Here's an example: At a fund-raising event, Mark read the palm of a woman named Gina in her forties. The area on the side of her hand just beneath the baby finger was crowded with nearly a dozen horizontal and vertical lines, some very deep, some almost too fine to see. It turned out she had never been married and was quite definite about never having had children. "Actually, I wouldn't have time for my own children," she laughingly told Mark. "I'm too busy with other people's children." Gina had owned and operated a daycare for nearly twenty years, an occupation that was, for her, plain heaven. Her daycare was extremely successful. Why? Because Gina was so much more than an employee paid to baby-sit other people's children. She was, to all intents and purposes, acting as a mother to all the children she took care of. She adopted them in a very real and meaningful sense. And they adopted her; some of them would come to see her years after being her charges at the daycare. Thus this woman who had no children of her own really had scores of children—and the relationship lines to prove it.

Whenever you find these relationship lines on the side of a hand that you're reading, let the person down gently. No, these lines won't tell young women how many children (or husbands!) they will eventually have. The good news is that it's up to them. What these lines tell us is how many truly important relationships we will experience in the course of our lives. And isn't this a much more important number to know?

# What the Mounts Say About You

In this chapter we'll take a look at the classic mounts of modern palmistry: specifically what the Jupiter, Saturn, Apollo, Mercury, Mars, and Venus mounts say about personality strengths, energy levels, and talents. The mounts are the fleshy areas located at the base of the fingers—usually raised areas that make most palms a rolling landscape of pillowy ups and downs. Mounts are the reason that—when you hold your hand out in front of you, level, in a relaxed manner—the very center of your hand forms a somewhat sunken region that looks just perfect for holding a baseball (or crystal ball).

# Locating the Mounts

Looking down at your palm, imagine that it is a wide plain ringed by mountains. At the top of the palm, where the fingers begin, you'll see a mount for each of the fingers:

- Under the index finger you'll find the Mount of Jupiter
- Under the middle finger you'll find the Mount of Saturn
- Under the ring finger you'll find the Mount of Apollo
- Under the baby finger you'll find the Mount of Mercury

The size and location of the mounts can give us information about a person's potential and interests—so let's take a closer look.

# Individual Takes on the World

The mounts allow a person in the know (you!) to get a quick snapshot of where someone puts the emphasis in her life. They can also be a map to hidden treasure—unrealized potentials and talents. Each mount gives us a unique perspective. You'll learn to use them to see where the palm's owner places her interest and how much energy she has to follow that interest. You'll be able to locate the areas of life a person is most public about, and in which areas she tends to want more privacy. Knowing where a person's interests lie can reveal a lot about the way she deals with the world. The mounts can give you a lot of information, very quickly.

## "Flat" Palms

Some palms are almost flat with what seems like very little padding. But if the owner cups his hands, just a bit, you should notice that some areas stand up a little more than others. These are the features, the mounts, you will read. They say that still waters run deep. The people with palms that are flat and sometimes very smooth are those people with unsuspected depths, and sometimes very private selves and lives. These people are often gregarious, outgoing, and extremely social. Nevertheless, they keep a certain portion of their inner lives discrete—for themselves and just a few others whom they've known for years, people who are on a short, select list.

# Mount of Jupiter

The first mount we'll look at is the Mount of Jupiter. This mount is directly beneath the index finger. Both the index finger and the Jupiter Mount are about how you announce yourself to the world at large, how you present yourself to the public for public consumption.

If your Mount of Jupiter is directly beneath the index finger and prominent—that is, raised— you are outgoing, very comfortable about being in public. Maybe you should consider running for office? You are quite capable of managing projects and taking praise that is aimed directly at you.

If the Jupiter Mount seems to have wandered off and is situated between your index finger and your middle finger and it's prominent, then, while outgoing and comfortable in public life, you are happier being part of a team. When the praise comes, you feel much more comfortable when it is aimed at the team as a whole than when it is given directly to you. In situations in which you are singled out for specific praise (even if you feel you deserve it), you feel extremely uncomfortable and off balance.

# Mount of Saturn

This Mount of Saturn, located directly beneath your middle finger, is about community and duty. It's all about how you handle obligations—both to others and yourself. If this mount is prominent, you have a strong sense of community. You are the kind of person whose life is going best when you are involved with your family, friends, and local community with commitment and passion.

# Mount of Apollo

The Mount of Apollo, located directly beneath your ring finger, tells us about your personal creativity, the way you handle and process the world of symbols. It tells the reader about the way you use your imagination. And this mount tells us a lot about the way you make meaning in the world. Every perception is a creative act. This is the reason we all see not just one world, about whose nature we all agree, but many worlds—and we all see them in decidedly different ways. The Mount of Apollo tells us about you as a perceiver. Every one (even those who can see other people's creativity but are able to ignore or overlook their own) is a closet Leonardo, painting and perceiving the world for themselves and others in every word they speak and every activity and project they undertake. If the Apollo Mount is prominent, you will be deeply into creativity in some

nse of color and form and
c elements work together.

## of Mercury

ury is about how you com-
nal version and vision of the
is mount (like the baby fin-
have more importance for
palm readers than it had in
of palmistry. We live in a
y being transformed by communication—and this changes everything we
thought about this mount in days past, giving it a
new importance and relevance. To understand
this mount, you need to think in broader ways
about the nature of communication. Yes, communication is about the ability to speak, to weave
webs of words, the ability to make your point
clearly, even at times, forcefully.

But communication is also much more than
that. To understand what the Mount of Mercury
means in the modern sense, you need to think in

big-picture terms about it. Today, the Mount of
Mercury is about cell phones, multimedia, hyper-
text, satellite television, Internet and intranet, data
encryption, and e-business happening 24/7. If
the Mount of Mercury is prominent, if it rises
from the general flatness of the palm and distin-
guishes itself, then you are an outstanding com-
municator *in some sense*. You may be a master
schmoozer, with an ability to connect with others
quickly and to maintain those connections—
sometimes over years.

At a recent event we met Stephen. He had a
prominent Mount of Mercury and an ability to
make people comfortable almost instantly, to make
strangers friends in a matter of moments. He is
phenomenally effective in this regard. We watched
him call an 800 number to inquire about getting
a defective part returned and were amazed at his
skills.

People who answer toll-free customer-service
numbers and deal with return requests can be very,
very defensive. Their job is to field phone calls
from irate customers. These folks are use to having the people they talk to go nuclear on them.
Yet in less than five minutes, Stephen, the master

schmoozer, had gotten the customer service rep to agree to send a replacement part by overnight courier and to pay for the shipping costs. Stephen and the service rep were joking, actually laughing on the phone by the time the conversation was over. How did our master schmoozer manage to accomplish this feat? As soon as he had the customer service rep on the phone, he said: "You know, they sometimes record these phone calls, don't they?" (Of course, the master schmoozer knew this, because he'd just been informed of the fact moments before, by a recorded voice.) "Well," he said, "I know that we'll feel a *lot* more comfortable if we're on our own. So"—he paused—"I'd like to request that no recordings be made of our conversation. Can I do that as a customer?"

From then on the conversation was one between two human beings who might become friends—two people who were interested only in helping one another out.

Now, that is Mount of Mercury magic. Two human beings linking up to assist each other, acknowledging that they are part of the same web.

We have to admit to a sneaking affection for the Mercury Mount. Let's face it—in a world where one can spend hours every day just responding to e-mail, communication skills are a much needed commodity.

# Mount of Venus

The Mount of Venus is located directly beneath the thumb, and for most people it's the largest of the mounts. More than any other mount, this one has to do with the human basics: your vitality or life force. It will also reveal whether you are most concerned with the inner world or the outer one.

If your Mount of Venus is prominent (we think of it as well pillowed) then many of your concerns will be in public life—with what you do for a living, with family and friends, and with the activities that make up your day-to-day life. And you will feel supremely comfortable living your life this way, with lots of activities to enjoy, tasks to juggle, and commitments to meet. This is where your satisfactions lie.

If your Mount of Venus is less prominent or almost flat, it indicates that, while you are likely to have commitments aplenty in the great world, you are singularly drawn to the interior world. In the past, these people have been called introverts, but something more (and certainly something more interesting!) is happening here. Those with a low Mount of Venus are adept at exploring the world from a deeply intuitive perspective. They tend to have more frequent encounters with their intuitions ("someone I haven't heard from in a long time is going to call today"), and their hunches often turn out to be correct. They're also known for their thoughtful and compassionate ways and have deep empathies.

If your Mount of Venus is not padded, you are able to feel the ups and downs of friends and family—not simply an intellectual recognition of their triumphs and despairs, but a full-on connection that makes you capable of the very deepest friendships. When someone is in crisis she'll come to you, because you'll be able to understand her trials and tribulations in a way that few others can.

We've seen people with this feature nod their heads vigorously when we talk about this quality because they've been there and done that—usually many times. We tell them to be careful. They're so good at the soothing, the empathizing, that some people grow overly fond of the comfort they speak. They come to spend the night—and stay the month. We say be careful to support family and friends, with generosity, yes, but help them get back on their own road just as soon as they're able.

# The Worry Wart Grill

What's the Worry Wart Grill? It's a series of criss-crossing lines toward the bottom of the Mount of Venus—as if someone had thrown a fishing net across the palm. The Worry Wart Grill indicates that its possessor is an avid worrier. This person worries even when there is nothing to worry about. The thought process goes something like this: "Gosh, I pretty much defeated that last crop of difficulties. Looks like there is nothing—right now, at this moment in time—to worry about. Could that be true? Nothing to worry about? Could I be missing something?"

We confess that we both have this feature displayed prominently on our palms. And we have led happy and productive lives. You can, too.

Part of dealing with the Worry Wart Grill successfully and productively is to take yourself with a big grain of salt. It's beneficial to enjoy long siestas from the nittering, nattering little worries that life tries to bring your way.

Don't worry, be happy. And have some serious fun. After all, that's what *Palms Up!* palmistry is all about.

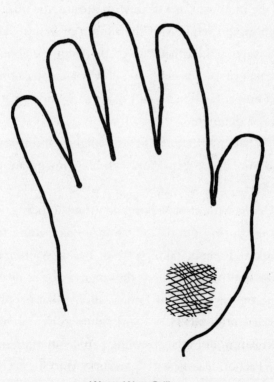

**Worry Wart Grill**

# Mount of Luna

Last (but you'd better believe not least) is the Mount of Luna. You'll find this mount located at the bottom half of the wrist on the baby finger side of the palm. We find it the most interesting of the mounts. Luna deals with dreams, the imagination, and symbols. If the Mount of Venus—all the way on the other side of the palm—is about matters of the daylight—energy, vitality, passion, and empathy—the Mount of Luna is about matters of the night.

What are matters of the night? Intuitions and hunches, dreams and symbols, imagination and art.

If the Mount of Venus is about what individuals do during the daylight hours—like going to work and school, taking care of business, looking after the future—then the night world dealt with by the Mount of Luna is about what people do after the world of work is done. It's about daydreaming. In daydreaming people set out (and sometimes complete) journeys they'll never actually take. Luna rules over the dream life—and over everything in life that's mysterious, all things that make sense without making sense.

If you have a prominent Luna Mount, you have the uncanny ability to connect with others through the poetic, through the use of metaphors and analogies. This is the way we think of the kind of powerful communication that the Mount of Luna represents: It's the difference between a photo of the bombing of Guernica and Picasso's huge work that depicts the same thing.

If you sport a prominent Mount of Luna, you are remarkable for recurring dreams, the sort of sleep-images that come back to you at night over long periods of time, some since childhood. You may be characterized as sensitive, someone who has experienced some of humanity's oddest experiences: knowing events before they occur or being aware of happenings that you should have no way of knowing about, for example, seeing people after they've shuffled off this mortal coil. We've noticed that when we mention this to people with a prominent Mount of Luna, they are often relieved—and sometimes tell us the very oddest things, experiences they've had over the years that they've never told another living soul about. Until now.

# Mounts Directly Beneath the Fingers

Sometimes the mounts will be located directly beneath the fingers they're associated with. The Jupiter Mount will be directly beneath the index finger; the Saturn Mount will be directly beneath the middle finger, and so forth. When this occurs, the person's mounts are telling you that the characteristics represented by that mount's finger are straightforward, direct, and full of energy. It also means the person has the skills (whether they realize it or not) directly associated with those mounts.

Do you have a mount located directly beneath . . .

- Your **index finger**? This is the Jupiter Mount. You will have skills and characteristics directly related to leadership. Think about running for office!

• Your **middle finger**? This is the Saturn Mount. You will have skills for working together with people in a community setting. You will also have a deep sense of history, tradition, and duty. Volunteer for something—today. You can achieve great things for groups you are a part of.

• Your **ring finger**? This is the Apollo Mount. A mound beneath the ring finger means that you have skills and potentials in the world of art. You have a fine aesthetic sense—and a flair for the original. Although artistic skills take time to develop, they pay off big in benefits to you and the people closest to you. No time like the present to dust off that digital camera and enroll in a class. You've got an eye for color and design. Time to use it!

• Your **baby finger**? This is the Mercury Mount. You are keen on communication. You are a good talker, storyteller, or salesperson; you can think on your feet and entertain those around you with style and wit. But forget about shutting you up! Once you're on, you're on. If you've got this bump happening, we suggest you audition for a spot on the local television news. You're a talker who's looking for a place to speak from.

# When the Mounts Aren't Directly Beneath the Fingers

Some people have mounts that are located not directly beneath the fingers with which they are associated but on one side or the other. Here's where things get interesting. These "wandering mounts" will give you a perspective on the nuances of their owners' characters.

# A Mount Between the Index and the Middle Fingers

If you've got a mount that looks like it's located between the index and the middle fingers, most palm readers will go cross-eyed trying to figure out whether it's a Jupiter Mount (supposed to be located just below the index finger) or a Saturn Mount (associated with the middle finger). Trouble yourself not, *Palms Up!* reader. When we find a rising mound of flesh between these two fingers, we know that the mount has to do with a synthesis of the characteristics found in the two mounts: leadership and community.

You have enormous reserves of optimism and energy. At your very heart's core, you tend to be an optimist with a deep-seated belief that if we all pull together we can make a better world. When we say *optimist,* we do not mean that you are impractical, that life is a champagne and roses affair. You are also a realist who believes that the people in a community can pitch in to create a worthy future for themselves and their neighbors. As you mature you'll season your skills in this area. You probably volunteer for community and charity work. You are a doer not just a talker.

## A Mount Between the Middle and the Ring Fingers

If you find you have a mount between your middle and ring fingers, you will have a deep sense, sometimes conscious, sometimes not, of the way that art and creativity binds a community together. The equation Community + Art = Culture will be deeply embedded in your sensibilities and activities. To you, art and community are one, indissoluble, till death do them part.

## A Mount Between the Ring and the Baby Fingers

If you have a mount between the ring and the baby fingers, you are concerned with artistic sensibilities and communication. You are a great storyteller and dynamic salesperson. This mound announces that creativity and communication are well developed in you. You are a fascinating companion at dinner, able to keep the crowd at a table spellbound with tales of your life and the lives and adventures of your acquaintances.

Beware, however, because, as a possessor of this mount, you can grow entranced by the sound of your own voice, and you've been known to embellish a tale or two just for the added exuberance it will give the telling. The truth is never strict for you, and the facts seem to get larger with every telling. But no one seems to mind. And the reason no one seems to mind is that you have abundant charm, most often exemplified by the way you speak and the tales you tell, but often in other ways of communicating as well. Body language, facial expression, hand gestures—you tend to use it all and use it effectively.

# How to Look at the Mounts

A famous Greek philosopher said, "Know thyself," which seems like a good place for the *Palms*

*Up!* reader to start. Like a talented, dedicated, and ethical physician, we're going to start with ourselves. Bring your palm up in front of your face— a little higher than usual and a little closer, so that the palm is four or five inches from your nose. Next, tip your wrist so your fingers move away from you and you're looking across your palm, as if you were looking across a tabletop at eye level. Do not bend your hand so far back that it is painful. Looking across your palm this way will give you a good vantage point for looking at your mounts. You're looking for the qualities we've described, especially for details like these:

- How high are the mounts? In this case high means more—and extraversion. Low means introversion or that the quality of the mount will be more introspective, meditative.
- How soft or hard are the mounts? A soft mount will emphasize the emotional, warmer side of human nature. A harder, firmer mount can be read as a more intellectual quality expressing itself.

• What are the mounts positions? Where the mount is located will determine whether it has the straightforward qualities associated with the mount or whether it's a blending of the qualities of two mounts.

# The Four
# Hand Styles

If you've read any other books on palmistry, you may have heard of the four hand types: water, fire, earth, and air. We're going to talk about these hand styles, too—bearing in mind that, more than anything else, these hand attributes affect our lives as style *choices* not as facts carved in stone. Another way to look at it: Some people like to read mysteries, others like science fiction. This does not mean that they don't enjoy other kinds of reading. This is the way it is with the hand styles; the shape of a hand gives the palm reader a glimpse into the *general* style of individuals, how they prefer to move and handle themselves in the world.

# Your First Reading

Now that you've journeyed this far in the world of *Palms Up!* palm reading it's time to put your skills as a palm reader into play in the real world. Remember, everyone gets butterflies the first time she offers to read someone else's palm. But your case of nerves will depart quickly when you realize that almost everyone is thrilled to have her palms read.

The best way to approach people is honestly. Tell her that you're learning how to read palms and would like a chance to practice on her. In our experience, no one has ever said no. In fact, most people—who have only heard about the experience, read about it in books, or seen it in movies—will act as if you were doing them a kindness. They will be thoroughly entertained.

And that's the way to view the experience—as

entertainment. It's best not to take on a super-serious attitude. Also, as a modern-day palm reader, it's your responsibility to remind the person whose palm you're reading that she is a unique creation of nature, and that she is doing you a favor.

A favor? Yes, by letting you hold her palm, enter her world, and gain practice and skill in the art of palm reading, she is allowing you to get close in a way that people rarely do. It's good to respect that intimacy by being gracious, respectful, and positive.

How do you hold someone's hand for palm reading? Ask her to hold out her hand, palm up. Take hold of the hand with both of your own (gently, now!). Hold her hand by the edges, with your right hand grasping hers where the index finger joins the palm. Your left hand grasps the hand where the baby finger joins the palm.

You'll be surprised at how quickly and easily you become comfortable taking people's hands into your own.

# The Water Hand

Water Hands are passionate, flexible, unafraid of diving in and experiencing life firsthand. The Water Hands will be the first on the block to have experiences that are exciting, different, and deep. Sound like you or anyone you know? Let's take a look at your palm. If you're a Water Hand, two things are true:

- You have long fingers
- You have a long, rectangular palm.

The Water Hand has often been called the *psychic hand*. Water Hand folks think with their feelings; they feel the rightness or wrongness of a proposition without any conscious reasoning at all, but rather with intuition. Most hand types do this at times; Water Hands do it more than most.

What is *intuition*? Books have been written about it, but the fact is that intuition is one of the least understood of all human thinking styles, and it is heavily influenced by the right hemisphere of the brain. While the left hemisphere gives people the ability to use language and perform feats of logic, the right hemisphere of the brain supplies us with such necessary skills as telling one face from another and other feats of pattern recognition (damage to the right hemisphere of the brain can prevent people from recognizing faces). In 1998, cognitive psychologist Gary Klein published the book *Sources of Power: How People Make Decisions*. It was the result of his decades-long study of the way people in under-fire situations make the decisions that either save lives or lose them. In his study, Klein concluded that, far from making their decisions by thinking through and weighing alternatives, when they're under fire, people—from paramedics to fighter pilots— make their key decisions by their subconscious, by their intuitions. Thinking based on intuition is remarkable in that it is based on metaphors and analogies rather than on complex and methodical heuristics of the kind that are used to solve problems in mathematics and logic.

Water Hands think in analogies and metaphors. The right hemisphere of the brain is responsible for a great deal of the senses of aesthetics and creativity. Intuition and aesthetics are deeply linked. While the left hemisphere speaks and thinks in words, the right hemisphere speaks in symbols. The right hemisphere of the human brain is the origin of the symphonies of Mozart and Stravinsky, the haunting images of Picasso and Georgia O'Keefe, the poetry of Emily Dickinson and Adrienne Rich. Most Water Hands will have at least an interest in the arts. Many will be practitioners of some art form: music, painting, or poetry.

One of the terms that deeply intuitive people are given is *sensitive*; they are more open to the influences of their environment than many others. Because of this, more than any of the other hand types, there are times when Water Hands need to be alone. Water Hands need to recharge their batteries, and they seek out peaceful environments that do this for them. If you want to do something particularly nice for a Water Hand, consider giving him a certificate to a day spa. They respond more than other hand types to rest and relaxation in an environment free of jarring noises and colors. Water Hands will thank you for treating them to a deliciously decadent pedicure;

and as the feelings of Water Hands run deep, you can expect their thanks to be lavish.

More than any other type of hand, Water Hands will be interested in ecology—all kinds. The sensitive part of their nature, their openness and sensitivity to the world around them, make them feel deeply about almost everything in their world. They are passionate about the causes to which they give their support.

Water Hands are always interested in others, not only in what those others are currently doing but the way they *feel* about what they're doing. Water Hands are curious about the way their own feelings interact with those of others. This may make them appear to be gossips at times, but the truth of the matter is that they are genuinely interested in the emotional lives of others.

# The Fire Hand

The wielders of the Fire Hand are a dramatic, energetic lot. They have longish palms, but shorter fingers. The shorter fingers indicate that they are not into details, but they do have quick minds (and, usually, tongues!) that enable them to mesmerize people with tales of their exploits. Fire Hand folks love to travel. To determine if you're a Fire Hand, look at your palm:

- You have short fingers
- You have a rectangular palm, longer than it is wide

The Fire Hand is the hand of overachievers who like their life full and brimming. This means that the average Fire Hand leads a pace that is brisk, to say the least. Fire Hands are full of invention and fun, happiest when deeply involved in projects that will have an impact on the world at large. The typical Fire Hand prefers the big picture and likes to leave the details for others. Fire Hands love an audience and will go out of their way to acquire one. Public speaking has been cited as one of people's biggest fears—Jerry Seinfeld quips that most of us would rather be in the coffin than delivering the eulogy. But this is less true of Fire Hands.

Most Fire Hands folk possess a dramatic flair that makes public speaking a breeze; you'll find a good share of Fire Hands in professions that make use of the dramatic. The average Fire Hand craves a world full of stimulation. Although it's not exactly impossible to find this environment in country life, many Fire Hands crave an environment that is stimulation-rich, leading them to prefer city life.

The modern world of advertising was made for the Fire Hand. Everything is supersized, ultrashiny, and—most of all—brand new. You'll find many Fire Hands drawn to the world of high technology, where the promise of a fast-changing world is an exciting prospect. Because of the Fire Hands' appetite for novelty, they frequently find themselves drawn to the latest and greatest gadgets: the first camera/cell phones, PDAs, MPEG players, recumbent bicycles. Their appetite for newness means they are frequently the early adopters, the first on their block to own one of anything new and different.

Fire Hands (more than any other hand shape) are natural-born optimists. Since they're very active and not into detail, you might accuse them of looking at the world through rose-colored glasses. You'd be close. But rose colored is not quite accurate. The glasses that this hand type sees the world through are fire-tinged. And because of their ability to see life on the upbeat, Fire Hands are a natural antidote to a case of the blahs. People with this hand shape always have projects in the works, projects that they are excited about and, more important, want you to become excited about.

With so much to do and be, there is no time (or room) for long-lasting fits of depression. Fire Hands look to the future because in their minds that is where the fun (and the action) is. Fire Hands have an almost magical ability to set the world around them in motion. Fire Hands make things happen.

The downside of this quality is that Fire Hands are prone to impatience and have a low (incredibly low) threshold for frustration. If you really want to frustrate a Fire Hand, inundate her with details. Her nervous system will cry out, enough is enough, and the boiling point will be reached. Then you will find out why some people are described as having a "fiery" temper.

Craving novelty and excitement as they do, Fire Hands give short shrift to activities that bore them. For example, in the realm of entertainment, when most people see a movie at the local theater, they'll remain in their seats and give the film every conceivable chance to divert them. Not so, Fire Hands. They will give a film about twenty minutes to wrap them in its silvery trance. At the twenty-minute mark, they will begin to get restive and start fidgeting in their seats. At twenty-five minutes, they will rise, popcorn cup in hand, and make their way toward the exit sign, with vague disgust written on their faces. There are better places to go and better things to do.

For the most part, Fire Hands make decisions quickly, and these decisions are made on the basis of intuition (for women) or gut instinct (for men). Because Fire Hands like to do everything in life at a fairly brisk pace, they don't spend a lot of time mulling over their choices; they are more impetuous. Enter, the hunch: That feeling of rightness or wrongness about a situation or decision serves our fiery folks well.

A good example of the Fire Hand intuition is found in Roy. The skipper of a fishing boat, Roy has an uncanny ability to take his crew where there are fish to be had—consistently. So much so that he is often shadowed by other fishing boats, wanting to get their nets where they can benefit from Roy's eerie ability to go where the fish are swimming.

Although Fire Hands crave the warmth of home and hearth, they will be somewhat allergic to any relationship that threatens to trap them in a static, unchanging situation. Although they like the idea of stability, Fire Hands are wary of the reality. Fire Hands crave relationships with active types—and they love surprise and adventure. Companions who seek a comfortable, stay-at-home existence with little change or stimulation will be unable to keep the interest and affection of a Fire Hand. On the other hand, if you like the idea of a fast-moving relationship, with the top rolled down and the music played at a high volume (even if it is Beethoven), this may be just the sort of hand style that will appeal to you.

Every hand style has one thing that it's most fearful of. Thinking metaphorically, ask yourself, does Fire fear the extinction offered by Water? Does Air feel leery of the smothering it might suffer at the approach of Earth? Perhaps this is a strange way to think, but it's very much the way that the tradition of palmistry leans. For the Fire Hand, the fear is the fear of being completely, boringly, ho-hummingly average. Nothing dramatic there. Fire Hands are absolutely and inconvertibly 100 percent allergic to being considered average. A fate worse than death. Call the Fire Hand normal, and you might as well have dropped a bucket of ice water on him from a very high height.

The words most pleasing to Fire Hand sensibilities are words like *most, best, extreme,* and *extremely.* Pile on superlatives, and you will be surprised at how Fire Hands will glow and warm to you. So deeply do Fire Hands crave to be nonordinary, we've even known them to cuddle up to someone who flatters them with negative superlatives, implying (in the nicest way possible) that he is the very worst, the most vile of those that inhabit the earth.

If you want to flatter a Fire Hand, tell him how distinctive and unusual he is and how absolutely unlike anyone who's ever walked this earth before. Tell him he has, for once and for all, upped the ante on what it is to be a human being. He'll love you for it.

# The Earth Hand

Earth Hands are the great doers of life. To Earth Hands, the only thing that truly matters when all is said and done are the projects finished and brought into being, the list of accomplishments that are their legacy and serve as tangible evidence of the work they've done. This desire for accomplishing real work seems ingrained in the DNA of those who possess Earth Hands, forming the absolute bedrock of their being. If you are an Earth Hand:

- You have a square palm.
- You have short fingers.

In the past, books on palm reading have tended to give the Earth Hand fairly modest praise, seeing this important hand type as something less creative than some of the other hand types. But we twenty-first-century palm readers see the Earth Hand a bit differently.

Earth Hands are scorekeepers—not only with others but with themselves as well. They work hard and expect others to act accordingly. They crave accomplishment, but in a much different way from some of the other hand types. Earth Hands—more than any other hand type—care very little for public acknowledgment or praise for the things they do. While not allergic to public acknowledgment, the acclaim of the public at large does not motivate them like some of the other hand types. What does interest the Earth Hand are projects completed in the day-to-day world, a constantly growing list of accomplishments, of effort expended, of changes made in the world that these individuals are part of.

Earth Hands are natural-born résumé builders. They believe they have been put here on the planet to make additions to the list of human accomplishments. Because of this bias, Earth Hands are very focused. While not completely uninterested in the variety of experiences and emotions that life offers, they believe they can explore that variety on their down time (if they ever have any). They believe that actions are more important—much more important—than mere words or feelings about things happening in the world.

Earth Hands are action hounds, but not in the thrill-seeker sense. They aren't primarily interested in skydiving, extreme snowboarding, or the other activities done expressly for the purpose of tricking the nervous system into an adrenaline high. Although Earth Hands involve themselves in work on projects that produce a fair share of adrenaline highs and endorphin rushes, this is not the reason they pick the projects. No, Earth Hands are primarily interested in a process, a simple, practical one. They long to engage the world on its most practical level, to take the raw materials that life presents them with and make something or change something. Earth Hands are all about building, fashioning, and finally completing whatever task is put before them. At the end of every project, an Earth Hand wants to end up with a finished product—a product she can point to and say, "I made that."

Would it surprise you to know that Stephen Spielberg, creator and director of such record-crunching mega-hits as *Jaws, Indiana Jones,* and *Jurassic Park,* is an Earth Hand? Yes, this director, who seems to have a boundless appetite for wild, imaginative cinematic flights, is also a dedicated, hardworking drone devoted to bringing his complicated films in on time and on budget. Although Spielberg is often portrayed as a dreamy visionary, his résumé seems to belie this image of the man and the filmmaker. In many photos of Spielberg, one can see clearly that he is a classic Earth Hand with short fingers and a square palm. He has the hand of a doer.

Earth Hands are interested in testing themselves against the world, in working on projects that require daily exertion to bring them off. While not always addicted to work in the workaholic sense, Earth Hands are more than willing to put their time and energy into the projects that most interest them. We view the Earth Hand a whole new way—not as in the past, when having a square palm and short fingers indicated a person who was primarily interested in physical labor and nothing but—as the hand of a doer, a person who, whatever other qualities of imagination and vision she might possess, is interested in action that leads to results.

Earth Hands, although slow to commit, make long-lasting friends and commit deeply. They should wear a badge that says, "Trusted Friend."

Should you become part of an Earth Hand's close circle of friends, and she decides to help you, you will be helped. She will not be dissuaded.

Earth Hands take their time in becoming true friends with others. The reason for this is that Earth Hands commit not just for the moment—or for any finite period of time—but for life. When they decide that you are their friend, which means that they may have known you for a good ten or twelve years, you will have been subjected to an uncritical but fairly thorough scrutiny.

Once an Earth Hand decides in your favor, you are family. It will be as if you'd always been a part of her family, a brother or a sister. You will be extended the privileges and rights afforded to true kin. Come in the house and feel a bit hungry? She'll be genuinely surprised that you didn't just make yourself at home, open up the refrigerator door and help yourself to last night's lasagna. But until you've endured the time of scrutiny, you may feel as though you were on the outside with the boundaries of the relationship clearly marked.

What is the deepest fear of Earth Hands? Wasting their precious time. Although Earth Hands have mastered the art of patience more than any of the other hand types, they are more than a little obsessed with the idea of accomplishing things. You've never seen someone truly antsy until you've been in the presence of an Earth Hand when one of her long-term projects is on the verge of failing, of falling through the cracks. Earth Hands have their eyes on the long-term, sometimes on projects that will take years to complete. Their deepest fear is to put years of effort into endeavors that fail to come to fruition, to have wasted their time on plans that don't make the scoreboard.

On the other hand, Earth Hands know how to relax. They excel at the ability to take it easy after a day of dedicated, organized work. Hospitality comes naturally to Earth Hand people, and they are masters of the art of entertaining others in a manner that allows friends to let their hair down and leave the workaday world behind, completely forgotten. Unlike Air and Fire Hands, who seem to run their lives on an excess of nervous energy,

Earth Hands have no problem unplugging the phone, lighting up the barbecue, putting a few cold ones on ice, and turning up the stereo. If you have an Earth Hand as a significant other, aiding and abetting her in the art of relaxation will gain you major points.

To some people Earth Hands can seem driven and somewhat judgmental. True to a degree, this observation doesn't tell the whole story. They do frequently evaluate the people closest to them in terms of where these others put their time and energy. Earth Hands rarely criticize, but they do have a tendency to dismiss those of us they deem to be fundamentally unserious. You can get no greater compliment from an Earth Hand than that she takes you seriously.

Earth Hands simply don't bother with people who live and play by rules outside their areas of interest. They are no more concerned with or interested in the doings of people outside their sphere of interest than we might be about characters in a seventeenth-century Russian play that was never translated into English. Such concerns would be so far outside their personal map of things that matter that it would fail to register on the radar. However, once you do get on the playing board of an Earth Hand (this may take some time), you will have passed a crucial test. Remember: Earth Hands don't judge you by the criteria that matter to most people in the world, such as your looks, the plumpness of your pocketbook, the sheer trendiness of your being. No, Earth Hands judge you by the measuring stick that matters to them: How you use your time and energy—what you do. Once you've gained their respect and trust, you'll never find more loyal, more trustworthy friends. Although most of us give lip service to the concept that one shouldn't judge a book by its cover, for Earth Hands, this is a way of life.

# The Air Hand

Coverage is the name of the game for Air Hand folks, but their kind of coverage is intellectual. They want to explore it all. If you are an Air Hand:

- You have a square palm.
- You have long fingers.

The Air Hand is first and foremost about the human intellect, reasoning, perception, and point of view. People with this hand style are—like Water Hand folks—very much into details. But unlike their watery sisters and brothers, they have a greater knack for organizing. Air Hands are almost as impatient as Fire Hands. Their idea of hell is to be stuck in an infinitely long line at the bank or supermarket without a book. They hate tedium and will go to great lengths to avoid it—even, paradoxically, putting up with back roads and circuitous routes, so they end up arriving only minutes faster than they would have if they'd waited their turn.

Air Hands crave stimulation and require constant novelty to be at their best. They like an ever-changing mental environment, one that will inspire them with new ideas. They tend to be excellent mathematicians and inventors. If you said it sounds as though Air Hands had nervous systems that are constantly percolating, you'd be correct. They are always looking for ways to put their energy into the world around them; they are innovators at whatever they do. This character trait becomes for them a lifestyle, an actual approach to the world. Because of this quality, many Air Hands find employment in niches like engineering, where they can use their skills in a quickly changing environment.

Because they crave novelty, Air Hands are usually addicted to an activity level—a mental activity level—that seems a bit extreme to the people around them. They will *always* be involved in too many projects for their own good and seem to actually thrive in an environment of constant deadlines and due dates. The pressure of being responsible for making things happen on time is not a drawback for Air Hands because they're good communicators, and they come equipped with a positive genius for organization.

We frequently find Air Hands involved in political campaigns. Why? Political campaigns are events that require fast thinking, fast responding in situations that are extremely fluid, to say the least. More than most, Air Hands hate captivity. While Fire Hands have a basic fear of being lumped in with the "merely ordinary," the Air Hand's greatest fear is the idea that they might have to settle for doing the same task or gazing out over the same maze of cubicles for the rest of his life. Just the thought of an existence like this makes an Air Hand's heart beat a little faster and gives him a sensation of vertigo, the kind of feeling we called the heebie-jeebies when we were kids.

Since Air Hands tend to be restless thinkers, they appreciate someone who can be a foil for their analysis of how-things-went-today, a receptive person they can bounce ideas off of. Air Hands look for those who can give as good as they get, so it's never a good idea to remain passive with them. Remember, they love mobility in themselves and others and pride themselves on their ability to be (and stay) adaptable. They are able to adapt themselves to even large changes in another's career and ways of thinking about the world. You never need to be afraid of losing an Air Hand's affection because you are constantly changing as an individual. The simple fact is that change intrigues him, and this quality of personality is one of the advantages of being with an Air Hand.

# Using Hand Types in the Real World

Now that you know your way around the hand types, let's unpack some ways of using this knowledge in the real world. How can the wily palm reader use her skill and knowledge of these different mental sets to her advantage? Here are a few examples of how you can use your newfound knowledge to spice things up and make your life more interesting.

## At a Job Interview

During a job interview, pay attention to the shape of your interviewer's hand and register whether he's a Water, Fire, Earth, or Air Hand. Once you've identified the hand type you can play (verbally) to that type's strongest suit. For Water Hands, make sure you mention how you *feel* about the work you do and the skills you've managed to put together. Water Hands will also be interested in how you feel about the work environment and your contribution to it.

If your interviewer is a Fire Hand, make sure that you're being as good an audience for her as you'd like her to be for you. A Fire Hand's life (even a job interview) is a performance, so play your part well. This hand type responds well to *enthusiasm* and *confidence,* just as we do to an actor who's confident in her part in a play or film. If there's any way you can add humor (or drama) to the interview, your Fire Hand interviewer will thank you.

The Earth Hand interviewer responds to *accomplishments,* to projects completed and skills mastered. Make sure that you have these at the tip of your tongue *before* you enter the interview situation with this hand type. Being concrete and specific about what you've done in the past will help you get on the right side here.

The Air Hand interviewer will want the *details*. Don't make this hand type have to dig for the information. Although he is quite capable of going for the tiny details he craves, you will impress him more if you offer this information without his having to ask for it. Because of his love of details, the Air Hand can frequently make those he is interviewing feel defensive—as if the person were being subjected to a kind of third degree; in reality, all this detail-loving individual is attempting to do is collect the facts he loves so dearly. The thing to remember here is, don't become defensive. In fact, if you can manage the feat, ask for details in return. Since this is natural for the Air Hand, he will respect and appreciate your questions. After all, that's what *he* would do in your situation. Try to create an information flow back and forth—the key to gaining respect in the world of the Air Hand.

## At a Party

Now that you know a thing or two about hand types and their preferences, it's time to take it to this weekend's party. One of the easiest (and most) entertaining ways to deploy your knowledge of the hand types at a party is to play matchmaker. First, take it as your goal to introduce two compatible hand types to one another. If you have a girlfriend who is a Water Hand, try to find a compatible companion among the other Water

Hands or Air Hands at the get-together. Once you've located a likely candidate, make sure you have a good introductory spiel worked out. Here's one that you can adapt to most situations:

"Did you know that you're a Water [Air] Hand? Ever had your palm read before? I read palms, and I'm trying a little experiment. As a Water [Air] Hand, I'm betting that you should be extremely compatible with my friend who's a Water Hand. If you'll spend just ten minutes together, and then tell me if I'm right, I'll read your palm for you."

Once word gets around that you're matchmaking based on palm reading, you'll generate immense interest. Take your "experiments" seriously. Interview your participants afterward to see if they felt like they had an easy (or a difficult) time creating rapport with one another. Take notes, even if only mental ones, to fine-tune your sense of how the various hand types work together.

Remember these basic relationships: Hands of the same type relate easily to each other: Water Hand with Water Hand, Fire Hand with Fire Hand, and so on. Water relates easily to Air and vice versa. Fire relates comfortably with Air. Earth and Water are natural combinations. When you pair up these hand types, you can look forward to easy, smooth-flowing results. This is all basic old-style palmistry.

As a *Palms Up!* palm reader (and matchmaker), however, you should try some more modern combinations. Try Fire Hands with Water Hands. While old-style books warn that such combinations are too oppositional, we've found that this kind of partnership can be deeply passionate and enduring. After all, there is a reason that opposites attract. In this case, the drama and changeableness of the Fire Hand can experience rich, new insights and emotional delights with the flowing, deeply feeling Water Hand.

Once you've gained some experience as a matchmaker for others, you'll want to give some of these insights a spin in your own love life.

# Fingerprints

We're going to admit right off that fingerprints are at the top of our list of the most fascinating factors in the world of palm reading. They fascinate because once you've looked at hand shapes, fingers, mounts, and the major lines of the palm, you're prepared to look at elements that can give the observant palm reader the finest details that grant insight into yourself and into others. There exists no one in the world exactly like you, even if you're an identical twin. This has nothing to do with the way you wear your hat or the way you sip your tea. Your fingerprints prove it.

Of all the people in this universe, only you have the set of ridges found on your ten dainty fingertips. Even more important, the fingerprints are one of the *only* features of the human body that does not change over the course of a human lifetime (we've already mentioned that the lines on your palm *do* change—sometimes dramatically—over the course of your years on the planet). This fact, the permanence of fingerprints over a person's lifetime, was established in 1892 when Sir Francis Galton (a cousin of Charles Darwin) published his groundbreaking work *Fingerprints*. The next stunner that Galton revealed is that *every human's fingerprints are unique*. No two sets alike. Even in identical twins. So let's take a look at ways to use these marks to tell us what's up with the person who possesses them. In the past, much has been written on fingerprints and how they relate to palm reading, some of it contradictory. In this chapter, we focus on the material that is most striking, that tells you the most about the person who bears a certain fingerprint on a certain finger.

# Fingerprints Are for Special Occasions

Because fingerprints are hard to see in anything but very bright light, you will probably save them for special occasions, perhaps when you've given a fairly comprehensive palm reading. You've told someone about what his fingers reveal, and you've given him a good tour of his Life, Head, and Heart Lines.

Now he wants more. And that's what the fingerprints are, that little something more that you give someone for letting you hold his hand—and touch his life.

## Whorls

You'll start with one of the more distinctive, least common fingerprint marks, the whorl. Whorls are circular fingerprints and look (at least to us) a little bit like a cross-section of tree: The whorl is composed of concentric circles radiating out from a central dot.

The whorl represents energy, creativity, independence, drama, and novelty. This person is so dedicated to attracting the attention of others that she will do *anything* to attract the attention of passers-by. With this kind of dedication, the chance is she will succeed. The whorl is one of the more rare fingerprints. We see mostly loops (probably the most common) and arches (a bit less so). When you see a whorl on someone's finger, it is saying, "There's something interesting here!"

Whorls are a mark of distinction, and when you find them, the first thing you do as a reader is ask, Where's the whorl, on which finger?

The whorl will tell you where big things are happening in a person's life, and it will also tell you in what area of her life she should look forward to something special. Once you've found a whorl, you need to consider that particular finger, since a whorl represents a kind of independence of mind in the area that finger represents.

**The Whorl**

# A Whorl on the Thumb

A whorl on someone's thumb tells you there is a unique quality in the way he makes decisions and in how he follows through with those decisions. (It might help to review the chapter on the thumb— remember Lookers and Leapers?) If the whorl is located on the thumb, you'll find that the person will be extremely independent when it comes to making decisions. Although he will listen to other people, when it comes time to make the decision, he will be assertive. It really doesn't matter here whether he's a Looker or a Leaper; when it comes time to make the decision, he will feel that it is time to move, to make things happen. Because he's so convinced, the thumb-with-a-whorl person will just move forward with all the power of a natural force like an avalanche.

Does this sound stubborn? Perhaps it is, because it grows out of an inner certainty that few ever experience. Once in a while, you'll hear someone say, "I'd like to be as sure of *anything* as he is of *everything*." This is the trait that person is talking about. This trait can make people natural leaders.

## A WHORL ON THE THUMB OF A LOOKER

If the person happens to be a looker (that is, if the bottom phalange of his thumb is longer than the top part of his thumb), the whorl means that, although he takes his good sweet time when making decisions, crunching the numbers, running the spreadsheets, shopping till he drops, and *never* paying sticker price for anything, he is possessed of a kind of intuition that helps him make uncanny use of his decision-making ability.

The whorl also indicates an unusual way of seeing the world and doing things in it. The looker who possesses this mark will usually make decisions in a different (sometimes radically different) manner from others. This is sometimes a sign of the merging of reason and intellect. Look for heavy coordination between left hemisphere skills (using logic, being methodical) with right hemisphere talents (pattern recognition, holistic thinking, intuition). People with these abilities can make their mark in the business world: They are players.

## A WHORL ON THE THUMB
## OF A LEAPER

On the other hand, if the person is a Leaper (a person whose thumb has a top phalange big enough to dwarf their bottom phalange), the sort of person who makes instantaneous decisions based on intuition or gut instinct and then uses copious amounts of willpower to bring them off, he will go through periods when he is exceedingly lucky, finding coincidence after coincidence to help him make his way through life with style.

## A Whorl on the Index Finger

If the person whose hand you are reading possesses a whorl on her index finger—the finger of the public self—look for something quite special in that arena. Is she a politician? This mark indicates that, just perhaps, she might think about running for public office. She will possess the dramatic, fiery qualities that enable her to get others excited about the same things she is excited about.

The whorl on the index finger also indicates that this person will be headstrong in picking the career she wishes to make her life's work. While other people might be intimidated by taking a radically different path from the people around them—deciding to become a speed skater, a musician, a big-game hunter, a fashion model—people with whorls on their index fingers will be headstrong about career choices. They're also not likely to listen to advice that they shouldn't go into this or that particular profession because it's risky and works out for only a few people in a million. They won't care. They consider themselves that one in a million. And, even more, they're willing to go to great lengths to prove it.

## A Whorl on the Middle Finger

If you find the whorl gracing the middle finger, you're looking at someone to whom the community, the family, the team, the company is more than just a part (like any other) of life. For this person the group *is* life—the thing that he works for; lives for; breathes for; sleeps, eats, and exists for. This is someone who is liable to be involved in a big way in volunteerism and in doing things for his community, church, school, and family.

In this category you will also find a good share of politicians and not a few lawyers. However, these lawyers and politicians will be less interested in pursuing their occupation out of a need for power and acclaim, but more because they truly and deeply want to be of assistance.

The keyword here is *service*. Those who have whorls on the middle finger have a positive need to be of assistance to other people. In this group you will also find teachers, doctors, and nurses. Because the whorl is about dramatic dedication, you will also find people who stubbornly must help those around them. These citizens won't take no for an answer. If they decide you need assistance, they will arrive on the scene (often with sirens wailing and cherry lights rotating) determined to be of help. You'll just have to live with that.

# A Whorl on the Ring Finger

If the person you're reading for has a whorl on the ring finger, you can expect her to come out with something special in the world of creativity. Here you find your natural-born entertainers and artists. To be honest, they don't exactly fit into the everyday world, because they are likely to see the world from a somewhat novel angle, and they just can't keep their mouths, eyes, ears—

paintbrushes, instruments, word processors—shut about their visions.

On the other hand, they make the world prettier, more imaginative, more mysterious, and just flat-out more meaningful to the people around them. You'll never be the same after they've managed to put their weird and colorful thoughts, images, tunes, and ways of perceiving the world into your life.

Of course, they can also be somewhat savagely insistent about the visions they have. They want more, often much more, than a passive audience for their sensibilities. They will often be insistent that you climb aboard their tour bus and be a part of their magical mystery tour. So be warned.

# A Whorl on the Baby Finger

When the fiery individualism that the whorl represents is located on the baby finger, we're looking at someone who either has, or will develop, a very dramatic or distinctive way of expressing himself.

Remember: The whorl is a symbol of focus (doesn't it look a bit like a target?). At times, the focus can be extreme, reaching the point at which it tends to block out all incoming information, leaving the person with a satisfying sense of self-hood that leaves the rest of the world (even those closest to him) outside the picture frame.

Sooner or later, those who have a whorl on the baby finger develop a message. This is a private statement about some aspect of the world they feel driven to post for the entire world to see. The whorl gives the whorl-bearer the feeling that he is carrying an important piece of information (careful, don't drop it!) that he must get across to everyone he meets. It's what makes him (as an in-dividual) dramatic and distinctive. Those who possess this trait must remember to be patient with a world that never seems to take their mes-sage as seriously as they think it should.

## The Whorl and the Stubborn Streak

Are you getting the picture? The whorl gives di-rection and focus to the finger—and area of life—on which it appears, but it also adds a cer-tain drive. It gives a stubborn streak to the areas where it's found. Energy, yes. Focus, certainly. But you can also accuse these people of being just plain mulish at times. If they're honest, they'll admit they are.

If not—well, will it mean anything if I tell you they will *stubbornly* deny it?

# The Loop

You'll recognize the loop instantly by its shape. Imagine a slightly curving loop of thread lying in very clear water, disturbing the water slightly so that it sends out identical rippling reflections of itself. That's the loop.

The loop is the most common of finger markings, which is good for the human race in general. The loop denotes flexibility and adaptability— the number one qualities that made our ancestors survivors (and here we're *not* talking about the television show).

Think about it; it was flexibility and adaptability that enabled our great-great-great-great-grandparents to survive harsh winters, plagues aplenty, migrations by the boatload, famine, war, and pestilence—and the advent of reality-based television. And we wear the marks of this inherent, bone-deep flexibility on the tips of our fingers: the loop.

We call it a survivor's badge. Had we not this incredible talent for adaptation and flexibility we would now be chilling in the DNA hall of fame with our unlucky (and distant) cousins the dinosaurs, the dodos, the passenger pigeons, and the one-toed tree sloths—very noble, but very, very static. And although as human beings we know that the worst is always threatening, we are also capable of creating pocket paradises (paradises that include pineapples in the dead of winter and aspirin for our aches, be they head or body) because we've managed to survive so well with our uncanny adaptability.

So when some old-style reader of palms tries to tell you that you are average and unexceptional, just show them your badges and vote them off your private island! You're a one-of-a-kind, not-to-be-duplicated survivor; and the fact that you've got an absolutely custom-made set of calling cards on the tips of your fingers (and most of them will be loops!) proves it. Therefore when you read loops, point out that these markings indicate the wonderful and absolutely necessary talent for flexibility that we all need to be a survivor in this world.

**The Loop**

# Arches

The arch catches heck in many old-school books on palmistry. These books often heap scorn on the arch, even though metaphorically it is the item in the architect's tool box that keeps the gate from collapsing. The arch is also one of the fingerprint markings that's less common, more unusual. As you know, one of the principles of modern palmistry is that when you see a thing that's out of the ordinary, you pay close attention to it.

What does the arch look like? The arch is a series of lines on the pad of the finger that rise, sometimes gently, sometimes steeply, toward the center, and then fall away again. Imagine a mound or a low hill. It is unusual. According to a sample of 5,000 people taken by Great Britain's Scotland Yard, the arch is seen in less than 10 percent of all cases. This makes it the most rare of all the fingerprints. The arch is seldom seen, but often disparaged.

Here's our theory of why old-school books on palmistry took the time and energy to heap scorn on this feature: Arches are a bit edgy. When you look at the arch on a person's fingertip, this mark is telling you that in this area of life (indicated by the finger you find the arch on), there's definitely a tiger in the tank. These individuals may be meek; they may be mild. They may avoid speaking evil of their fellow citizens. They may be the kind of people who take pains to shoo a lost fly out of the house rather than reach for the flyswatter. Meek and mild, they may be—except for that one area in which they are not go-along, get-along people, where they will hole up in their own personal Alamo, come what may. In other words, in this one single area they're uppity.

And the uppity nature, this here-I-stand-and-draw-a-line-in-the-sand quality must not have gone over with old-school palmists. To understand this, we need to think back to the time when the early books were written, by highly educated (very much a rarity at the time), mostly male members of a mostly elitist upper-crust contingent that adopted an Apollonian demeanor when it came to interacting with others.

Apollonian? The Apollonian personality prefers classical music, fine wines, muted colors, and traditional (but expensive) clothes. These people deplore loud noises made for the sake of exciting rude emotions in the lower classes. They like all their books arranged on the bookshelf in alphabetical order, *please!* They desire all of life's corners to be rounded. They dislike edge—and, by the way, uppitiness.

The very idea that anyone might prefer life a little edgier than this, the idea that some might prefer to actually get up to their armpits in the organic *messiness* of this world we live in—horrifies them and makes them wonder just what in creation the motives might be. After pondering the matter for a moment, the only explanation Apollonian types can come up with is that what they are seeing is some kind of *atavism,* a kind of throwback to an earlier and much more primitive mode of being.

This is nothing new. Anytime someone decides to swim against the flow or be a bit more vocal than those around them, she always gets accused of having something decidedly and distinctly wrong with her mental machinery. Too much edge.

We're of the opinion that this is the reason earlier palmists gave the arch much less respect than it deserves. We also believe that the qualities represented by the arch—the stubbornness and outspokenness—are here to stay and very, very unlikely to vanish anytime soon or from any future the human race is likely to inhabit. And, far from being an indication that we should check the person who possesses it for signs of an overly prominent brow ridge and clues that she would prefer to walk on all fours, it is a necessary part of what makes us human, a major tool in the human toolkit.

So, what's up with the arch? The arch is earth.

Remember that we said the whorl is like the element of fire, bringing changeableness and drama? And how the loop brings the flexibility and adaptability of water into the finger where it sits? Well, the arch brings the centeredness, and the insistence on creating that is associated with the Earth Hand into a person's life.

In reading the arch, the reader needs to make a distinction between (at least) two different kinds of creativity: the earth kind and pretty much all other kinds. The world we live in usually looks at creativity as coming from the imagination and working its way out into the physical world. Everything, this point of view says, starts as an idea, a creative idea in the mind of the artist. And while this is generally true, it doesn't help us understand the kind of creativity that's denoted by our friend the arch. Earthy creativity.

As we pointed out when we talked about the different kinds of hands, Earth Hands make their life about progress, about the things they build and create in this world. For an Earth Hand to be happy at the end of the day, she has to feel

**The Arch**

that she's accomplished something—the more concrete the better. She likes to *see* progress. Although Earth Hands can get by on the knowledge that their work has somehow moved forward *conceptually* they'd be a lot happier with something tangible to show for the day's efforts.

So it goes with the arch.

## What Does the Arch Mean?

If you find an arch on the finger of the person you are reading, it is an indication that she is looking for tangible, real-world results in the area that the finger stands for. There will usually be some sense of urgency, a sense of insistency, about this desire. Tangible results, please. This insistence on results is why this characteristic has received such a hard time from old-style books on palmistry. The person with an arch has an agenda. And the possessor will have clear desires for accomplishment in the area of the finger you find the arch on.

If the person's desire for real-world progress and tangible results are not met, she will more than likely display some of the following traits:

visible dissatisfaction, annoyance, and even rudeness and the insistence that goals be met and results be obtained. Although she may possess great flexibility in other areas of life, she is unlikely to display much flexibility in the area where the arch is found. Because of her lack of flexibility, she is very apt to gain a reputation with other people, to be seen as attitudinal, uncooperative.

The old-style palmistry books look on this as primitive, forgetting for a moment, we think, that this trait of single-mindedly advancing one's cause was taken as a reason for dismissing most of the worthy social changes of the past century: racial equality, the women's movement, environmentalism. Almost all the leaders and supporters of these movements were accused of having a disregard for general propriety and custom and lacking good will toward their fellow beings. We are careful never to dismiss the arch as being primitive. Just as with whistleblowers, sometimes the arch has something important to say to us.

And we'll miss it if we don't take the time to have a good listen. With that said: let's take a listen.

## AN ARCH ON THE THUMB

If you find an arch prominently displayed on the thumb of the person whose palm you are reading, you can expect her to be vocal about her commitments and decisions. Here's a person who has a deep dedication to accomplishing things in this world. She will also be very deliberate about making decisions and, at times, might have just a few issues of control with a capital C. Her decisions will have as their goal some practical result, and she will be wary of others until she sees the results of their choices and decisions brought into being, made concrete. These people very often have a collection of honors, trophies, and medals because, popular or not, they stick to things until they get accomplished.

## AN ARCH ON THE INDEX FINGER

An arch on the index finger tells the palm reader that the person will have staying power and a certain amount of intensity when it comes to public life. Here is someone who—whatever the circumstances, whatever curves life throws at her—will be capable of weathering the storm. Very often, if the person also has a long baby finger, she will be capable of inspiring others. The kind of inspiration she gives will not always be of the gentle kind.

Those with an arch on their index finger will have a deep belief in the worthiness of the way the world works, and little patience for those who question the human place in it. It is not that they cannot understand the way other people see the world; they see it, and yet their own vision is so strong that they must organize their world around the way *they* see things.

## AN ARCH ON THE MIDDLE FINGER

Friends, family, and community—if you find an arch on the middle finger, this person will have as a central concern an agenda having to do with other people. The arch on this finger can transform a person into an effective project leader, a supervisor, or manager who possesses a deep dedication to the people who are part of his group. Someone said: "Every successful project becomes a conspiracy." And so it is. With an arch on the middle finger, you have someone who has a real devotion for working with the group he cares about most (sometimes many groups at once) to accomplish an objective. These people are ready to suit up and put themselves in play, but they will demand to see results. Because of their focus and insistence on results, these people can be in your face at times.

## AN ARCH ON THE RING FINGER

Many artists *think* about more projects than they actually accomplish. If you locate an arch on the ring finger (associated with Apollo and the arts), you will be talking to someone who wants to start, craft, and finish every endeavor she becomes a part of—at least on the creative side of life. If the person is a working artist, she'll be the kind of artist who puts career first, ambitious to make it in the often difficult world of fine or commercial art. As a part of the art business, she will focus not only on the art but also on the business side, lining up galleries for showings and clients for buying. She'll very often display a practicality and pragmatism that is not a significant part of our (pretty much inaccurate) modern picture of the artist as a person who—like some delicate hothouse orchid—needs a special environment. An arch on the middle finger indicates the kind of artist willing not only to create but also to be in-volved in actively marketing her work. If you study the world of art and literature, you'll know this is not an unusual personality type to find. The English writer H. G. Wells often suggested ways for his publishers to promote his books, in-cluding the idea of hiring a person to walk up and down the streets of London with a sandwich board to advertise Herbert George's latest work.

No matter where her creativity lies, a person with an arch on her ring finger will want to get credit for her ideas. Although some who have this feature are masters at concealing their feelings, it truly rankles them to have the key ideas that help put a project over the top or help a breakthrough occur be misattributed to some less-deserving soul. It is (to quote the prestigious Winston Churchill) a thing up with which they will not put. Want to end a friendship with your best arch-on-the-ring-finger soul mate? Take credit for one of her ideas. On the other hand, if you want to please your significant other who has an arch on her ring finger, just be completely scrupu-lous, meticulously careful to give her credit for the ideas she has that move things along (believe us, she will come up with some breakthroughs) and mention this in the presence of friends and strangers.

## WHAT IF I'M NOT AN ARTIST, BUT I HAVE AN ARCH ON MY RING FINGER?

Often, you will find an arch on the ring finger of a person who has not made a decision to pursue the arts. He will not be on the way to mastering a particular medium—painting, music, or dance— but will use his creativity in other ways. As a palm reader, try to look beyond the narrow definition of the arts and find the place where an individual's creativity expresses itself. Very often what you will discover is the truly unusual, the artistic where it is not usually acknowledged. Don't be afraid to pry. Sometimes you'll find real creativity in some of the most unusual places.

## ARCH ON THE BABY FINGER

We very often associate an arch on the baby finger with people who work in some flavor of media: television, radio, theater, or the Internet. The arch gives this person an edge in an industry that is about getting your point across and creating market share. The arch gives this finger of communication a supercharging, a willfulness, that makes the possessor charismatic and attractive as a spokesperson. Although she may struggle in other areas of life, her ability to communicate with others will be foregrounded.

# Conventions

No matter what finger you find the arch on, you'll find that those who have this mark on their fingertips have less than the deepest respect for the conventions by which most people live their lives. This does not mean that they will necessarily live unconventional lives. They may be bakers, bankers, and lawyers; pay their taxes on time; and work nine to five for five days a week—and in all ways appear to be normal citizens living normal lives.

But although they understand and live by the conventions of the rest of society, they will not necessarily respect them down deep in their hearts. And—like a wild child—they will break them without any sense of guilt or any trouble of mind because, after all, they are only conventions—conveniences necessary but not vital to living life or interacting with other people. To those who possess an arch on any of the fingers, conventions will always be *merely* conventions.

Like the speed limit. Can you admit that you break the speed limit at least sometimes? We're not betraying any deep and dark secret when we reveal that when we use I-5 near Seattle, we keep up with the flow of traffic. If we were to drive the posted speed limit, we'd find ourselves sitting like rocks in the river, with waves of cars passing by on either side. The speed limit: a convention.

Those who bear the arch on one of their fingers, by and large, do not break conventions to shock people; that's something others would do (and this is the way arch-bearers think of it) as mere exhibitionism—by people who have issues with authority, issues they need to work out. The person with an arch is interested in doing something, accomplishing results. Conventions are just conventions, to be obeyed when necessary. However, if they stand in the way of a project that needs finishing or something else of real importance to them—well, no time to stand on tradition!

Let's raise a glass to the arch—long disrespected, long vilified. Although their edginess in certain matters can kind of get on others' nerves, their edge comes in handy and moves things along quite nicely when things need moving. Salud!

# Sheila's Hand Games

Now that you've had a chance to explore the world of hand shapes, here's a great icebreaker that asks an entire group to explore each other's romantic potential and love life. The game can be played by any number of people, as many as a hundred (Sheila has done this many times in performances for corporate audiences). But whether playing the game with a score of guests or just one special other during a romantic *tête-à-tête* over Cabernet, you'll find the game a great strategy for getting closer to others.

The game works with the hand shapes and what they have to say about two of the most important elements of relationships:

- Who are you most compatible with?
- What ways of relating will keep the romance healthy and vibrant?

Older, traditional books on palmistry are not optimistic about certain hand shapes and their compatibility with others. These books take the approach that while Fire Hands and Air Hands are great combinations (with prospects of high compatibility), the compatibility of Fire Hands and Water Hands is very unlikely (fire extinguishes water, get it?) and should be avoided. As we said in chapter 1, we read the hands of *hundreds and hundreds* of couples at events, and we can testify that this older view is simply untrue. We've had the pleasure of seeing successful couples with *every* kind of hand combination possible: Fire Hands with Water Hands, Earth Hands with Air Hands—romancing with complete success, even after years of couplehood.

That said: *all* couples have their difficulties, and some of those difficulties will grow out of the fact that they have completely different ways of seeing the world and each other. But successful couples deal with the differences. More than just deal, successful couples actually seem to thrive on their differences in outlook and develop deep affections based on those differences. And that's what Sheila's game is all about—finding and celebrating the differences.

If it's just you and the person in the running for significant other, then you're ready to go. If not, try pairing people by any system that makes sense (anything fun). You can create dynamic duos using the alphabet or start with the two who've had the most Pinot Noir; you can compare overbites and create pairs accordingly—it really doesn't matter. Once everyone is in pairs, bring out some sheets of paper and some pencils or marking pens. They're going to use these writing instruments to draw their partner's hand shape.

- Have one person in each pair place the hand he signs checks with flat on the sheet of paper.

• Have his partner trace the hand. Yes, he will want to do it himself, but resist his offer. This game and experiment is all about compatibility, about working together.

• Once his hand outline has been drawn (and he's drawn his partner's), determine which of the four hand types their hands belong to.

Long fingers belong either to a Water Hand or an Air Hand: with a long palm, it's a Water Hand; with a short palm, it's an Air Hand. If the fingers are short, it's either a Fire Hand or an Earth Hand: with a rectangular palm, it's a Fire Hand; with a square palm, it's an Earth Hand.

All right, it's compatibility test time. Each person has drawn his partner's hand. You've determined whether their hands are Water, Fire, Earth, or Air Hands. Now it's time to analyze what this means in terms of their compatibility.

# Identical Hand Shape Relationships

If you've got the same hand shape as your partner (Water–Water, Fire–Fire, Earth–Earth, Air–Air), then compatibility is a cinch. There will be a natural congruence of viewpoints. You'll intuitively know what the other person is up to and be able to easily see his side in almost every situation.

The difficulty of identical-hand-shape relationships is in the times when there *aren't* identical takes on a matter, a decision, or a way to go. As we know from our daily lives, some of the biggest blow-ups and hottest, nastiest debates can come between two people who share almost (but not quite!) identical takes on an issue.

# Nurturing Relationships

The next relationships we'll look at are those that complement one another. Many of the hand styles—though different from one another—actively support the point of view and action style of the other hand style. Let's look at them.

## Fire and Air: A Torrid Combination

A Fire Hand and an Air Hand are a powerful and volatile combination. Fire has a positive need for air to maintain its very existence, and the dramatic and impetuous behavior of the Fire Hand personality can add excitement and spice to the life of those with a more analytical bent; for instance, those who live by the code of the Air Hand. Fire Hands are not into details; and because of their restless natures, they often fail to focus on the details that can help them avoid bad decisions. Air Hands, because they have an absolute enjoyment for organization, can derive real pleasure from adding an organizational flair to the life of a Fire Hand companion.

Can you admit that part of the fun of every relationship is the way another person can help you to see (and feel) the world in ways that you ordinarily would not? This principle works to great effect in Air Hand–Fire Hand couples. Since travel and new experiences appeal to both Air Hands and Fire Hands, their enjoyment of these experiences as a couple is a powerful combination of their individual pleasure.

Another benefit of this relationship is that Air Hands, very much detail-oriented and much more intellectually oriented than their Fire Hand companions, can often get inspiration from the deeply passionate, fully emotional approach to the world that is natural to Fire Hands.

### ADVICE TO THE AIR HAND (ABOUT YOUR FIERY PARTNER)

Life with a Fire Hand is going to be exciting, fast-paced and—at times—perhaps a bit more emotional than you may wish. The first thing to watch out for here is the Messies. What are the

Messies? The Messies are the state an environment achieves once the Fire Hand has had a chance to exercise his natural flair for rumpling up the world around him. Books left here and there (Fire Hands will often read two or three at the same time); the kitchen in complete disarray, because your Fire Hand partner suddenly decided to make a new and unusual dish that caught his fancy; the video collection spread throughout the living room and the den because someone had an urge to put together an impromptu "film festival" for the two of you to watch tonight, and then (in midstream) lost both inspiration and train of thought or got called away on important business. All of these are products of Fire Hand lifestyle and result in the Messies.

Air Hand to the rescue! You as an Air Hand have a good sense of organization. You'll take the time to make sure that you create a place for everything, and that every little thing (forever afterward) is in its place. Your Fire Hand partner has no such knack for minding the details that keep life in livable shape. In fact, your partner *may* feel at times that your gentle nudges toward orderliness are crimping the natural spontaneity of his constitutionally derived right to play all things fast and loose.

Thankfully, as an Air Hand you have such an intuitive sense of organization that you should (given a little time and commitment) be able to train your partner into more organized and (slightly) less nerve-wrackingly spontaneous ways.

Good luck.

ADVICE TO THE FIRE HAND
(ABOUT YOUR AIRY PARTNER)

A relationship with an Air Hand is a deep one for you Fire Hands. For one thing you're turned on not just by his body and looks (although the attraction is potent!) but by his restless mind. His creative way of seeing the world is a decided turn-on. You'll spend lots of time trying to unravel the mystery of your Air Hand companion's point-of-view as you interact with it. You'll find this exploration intriguing in a way that is both puzzling and seductive.

But to be honest, he's just not as hands-on as you are.

As a Fire Hand, a deep part of you demands to mix it up with the world in real-time, don't-just-stand-there-do-something terms. There will be moments when you'll have the nagging suspicion that your Air Hand partner would rather watch the roller coaster than ride it. Which makes you impatient (not a very far jump for you at any time!).

But hang in there. Although he may seem to put himself a hand's distance away from the action, you'll find he learns quickly and easily. Yes, life is more a thing of the mind for him than it is for you. And, yes, he takes just a bit of coaxing to get into the water and start swimming. But he is willing, and is just as restless as you are, but in his own way.

Of course, the organization thing he's got going . . . well, you'll just have to learn to live with that.

## Water and Earth: Flow and Stability

Water Hands and Earth Hands are a combination we see frequently. This combination is usually very stable and very complementary—that is, each partner truly gets something positive, something needed from the other.

As we've mentioned earlier, Water Hands tend to be emotional with feelings that run deep, charging the way these people see the world around them. But emotions, by their very nature, are unstable and can lead to a withdrawal from life in general.

Enter, Earth. Earth Hands lend a welcome stability and groundedness to people with the emotional tendencies of Water Hands, supporting and giving shape, direction, and purpose to what might become for the Water Hand an emotion-for-emotion's-sake way of life.

In Water Hand–Earth Hand couples you'll often find a real sense of shared values. Although the personalities of the couple couldn't be more different (the Earth Hand is extremely practical and oriented toward doing, whereas the Water Hand is all about sensibility and deep feelings), their combined outlooks tend to produce a powerful shared reality as each partner becomes deeply influenced by the other.

Because Earth Hands are so completely oriented toward doing and achieving things, they often seem to ignore (perhaps seeing as impractical?) the emotional side of living. A relationship with a Water Hand will soften and give meaning to an Earth Hand's plans and activities. From the other side, Water Hands often acquire something valuable when their lives are given specific shape by the plans and activities of the Earth Hand. A good match.

### ADVICE TO THE EARTH HAND (ABOUT YOUR WATERY PARTNER)

Although the combination of Water Hand and Earth Hand is a strong one, you Earth Hands will have some adjustments to make in managing a relationship with your Water Hand companion. For one thing, there's that emotion thing. As we've pointed out, Water Hands are comfortable with and depend on emotion more than any of the other hand types. Deeply intuitive, a Water Hand will feel your moods and sense your emotions. Even when you're not actually having any. Feelings, that is.

Playing the emotion card—or wondering about what you're feeling—will preoccupy the Water Hand's thoughts, and she will want to know how you feel about things. Sometimes, if your characteristic Earth Hand patience deserts you, this emotional interrogation will seem like the Mother of all Pesterings while you are busy in your Earth Hand life trying to simply accomplish something!

As an Earth Hand having a relationship with a Water Hand, you should treat the questions about your emotional life not as prying but as a welcome reminder to observe your inner state.

Why? To learn more about it. If there's one thing that Earth Hands are good at, it's bulling their way through on just about any task, project, or activity. Since Earth Hands are focused largely on doing, constructing, creating at all times and places, it's healthy for them to remind themselves (or in this case, be reminded) that absolutely everything in life has an emotional charge, an emotional dimension, that can be taken into consideration. Very often Earth Hand types are so focused on getting to the goal as a way of life, they forget that maintaining those good feelings along the way is what makes a career, a goal, and—most important—a relationship worth doing and having.

## ADVICE FOR THE WATER HAND
## (ABOUT YOUR EARTHY PARTNER)

Water Hand, at times your nose-to-the-grindstone partner will baffle you. He will become so enmeshed in his projects, so busy seeing that his worldly enterprises are one step closer to completion, that he will fail to lay hold of some of life's most important and never-to-be-repeated moments. Was there an anniversary to celebrate? *Did we plan on friends for dinner? Why are you looking at me that way?*

Your wonderfully capable Earth Hand partner, so adept at wrestling with the world and winning, will seem at times abysmally clueless about life's truly important moments and matters, moments of emotion and matters of the heart. You're bound to experience frustration at times as you compete for his attention with the countless details and deadlines that are a necessary part of his innumerable projects. You may even reach a level of frustration with his Earth Hand ways that makes you want to cry out, "Remember me— remember *us*?"

Take heart, Water Hand, because *heart* is precisely your gift, your role to provide in this Water

Hand/Earth Hand relationship—a sense of the true value of the emotional side of life. Without the emotional insights you provide, your Earth Hand's life is bound to be productive but arid, full of accomplishments that, although wonderful in themselves, are less than emotionally satisfying. Even the greatest accomplishments only acquire meaning from their shared human context. The Eiffel Tower, Taj Mahal, and the Parthenon are merely architectural structures when viewed without the historical and emotional resonance that surrounds them. But as symbols? As symbols, those buildings speak of romance, of national and cultural identity, of human style and striving.

The Earth Hand will tend to see only what's in front of him: the project that needs finishing, the schedule that must be met. He will often miss the emotional aspect of the world. But as a Water Hand, you never do. Deeply intuitive, you sense the emotional secret that whispers from the heart of the world and from the projects your partner is so obsessed with. You know the deeply emotional reasons why others, not Earth Hands, sacrifice so much of their valuable time and energy to be part of his projects.

He sometimes looks so closely at the "How?" that he may miss the "Why?" Your gift to your Earth Hand partner is to help him see how much emotion and intuition matter in getting things accomplished in the world.

Of course, getting him to see the emotional side of life—a side that is so obvious to you but so hard for him—will take time. Be patient. The most beautiful garden remains nothing more than a plot of earth until the water comes and feeds its growing things.

## Water and Air Hands

One of the most interesting relationships is the Water Hand–Air Hand relationship. The reason for this is that air is actually a part of water. Remember $H_2O$? Perhaps because of this, Water Hand–Air Hand relationships tend to be very close. Both hand types are characterized by long fingers, representing their fondness for details, though it manifests in very different ways.

Water Hands crave details for their own sake, amassing facts, memories, opinions, and opinions *about* opinions without any concern for ordering the results. Imagine a museum with rooms full of items, some ancient, some new, all collected in a kind of Ali Baba–style treasure room in heaps, in chests. Furthermore, imagine this treasure trove distributed through a warren of rooms that are connected by winding corridors forming a maze straight out of the latest Doom-like computer game.

On the Air Hand side of things, there is a similar love of details. However, Air Hands crave not only to collect but also to organize the information and details they amass. Picture a filing cabinet, meticulously organized, with labels for each section so that the person wishing to find something can do so quickly and easily.

The bond in the Air Hand–Water Hand relationship is strong yet volatile. The similarities between these two hand types are so striking that you wonder what they could ever find to argue about, yet with two people so basically alike, these partners are destined to take a lot for granted when they deal with one another. There's a tendency to love the same things and love them in nearly identical ways, which can lead to a sense of closeness that can appear to the outside world as nothing less than eerie.

We see such couples everywhere—they sit close together and, no matter how large the crowd, the dynamic duo seems set apart, isolated from those around them by the sheer strength of their togetherness. Sometimes (is this conscious?), they'll adopt the kind of behavior we associate with twins:

- They'll wear the same (or very similar) clothes.
- They'll have their hair cut in almost identical styles.

Strange? Yes, but in Air Hand–Water Hand relationships what appears to be operating is an identification that comes from similarities blending over time. Although these two hand types start out from different places, over time they adopt more and more similar habits, viewpoints, and personality traits.

Since the personalities of these hand types are actually extremely different, there's bound to be some thunder and, on occasion, some lightning. The friction comes from the moments when the assumed closeness breaks down, and the differences between the Air Hands and Water Hands are brought into stark relief.

## ADVICE TO THE AIR HAND (ABOUT YOUR WATERY PARTNER)

Organization—or rather disorganization—could be what's making your life difficult and your temperature (and blood pressure) rise. You have this relationship that's working out—really—*so well!* And yet there are these moments when the level of irritation reaches a danger point . . . we understand.

Water Hands will never be as adept at the systematic organization of the world and its myriad contents as you. You'll have to face that fact—the earlier in the relationship, the better. For your own sanity.

But one thing you should *not* forget, and you should focus on when his lack of organization drives you ever closer to the rubber Ramadas of this world, is the fact that no one can appreciate (and show his appreciation of) your Air Hand ability to analyze the world like a Water Hand companion. You may be a master of thought, a vast intelligence capable of sorting the world into its component parts, but you'll never have the insights into emotion and the ability to support someone else emotionally, not like your favorite Water Hand.

You share so much. Your Water Hand is interested in looking at the world in the same way that you are, but he's much more emotional about that world. And as an Air Hand, you can actually grow more than a little bit from experiencing that emotional and deeply aesthetic response to the world that your watery companion can give you. Although a bit disorganized to your way of thinking, the emotional (and deeply intuitive) response to the world out there may (and, in fact, probably will) lead you to insights you might not have—and probably couldn't get—in any other way.

So, Air Hand, when things get a bit disorganized might it not be worth your while to . . . lighten up?

Yes, just a bit, because, after all, relationships, when they retain their vitality, get sweeter, better, and more valuable with the passage of time. Forgive the completely bad metaphor here, but like real estate, relationships increase in value from an investment of both energy and time.

## ADVICE TO THE WATER HAND (ABOUT YOUR AIRY PARTNER)

Control freak! Admit it, at times these are the two words that you want to scream at the top of your lungs, when you want your partner to once and for all relax just for a minute and quit the everlovin' hassle he seems to be presenting you with.

Which is too bad, because in all ways, most days, most times, you seem to get on so well, with very few problems and lots of good times that far outnumber the seconds, the mere minutes of strife.

Are we right? You see, Air Hands are absolute masters of organization. They tend to be intellectual, attracted toward understanding and systemizing things. This makes them wonderful as scientists and deep thinkers. As a Water Hand you have a great affection for this side of his personality, but at times it can be just a bit much.

Water Hands and Air Hands are a good fit most of the time and make their way together (very nicely, thank you!) except for those moments when you feel like the other has become just a little too organization happy. Then it's time to call for a time-out.

Can't he *ever* take time to slow down and smell the roses?

Which is what your contribution to the mix can be. The world of the Air Hand, at times, can get just a bit intellectual, a bit dry, and even a bit distant. And that's where some of your strongest qualities can come in and make a difference, make his world less abstract, more sensitive to the emotional side of life. A little more soulful.

Adding this dimension to a relationship with an Air Hand is going to take some dedication, however. Be prepared for a bit of testiness on the part of your Air Hand other. He loves (and even craves) order and sometimes loses sight of the fact that the world is organic. All of it. A growing thing that isn't composed only of nice neat divisions that clearly separate the world's working parts into antiseptically clean compartments, nice tidy little packages (scientists call it quanta) of separated stuff.

Even the world of mathematics is beginning

to acknowledge this messy fact. In trying to do something as simple as measure the coastline of Great Britain, splendidly linear mathematics runs into problems difficult to deal with. An entire branch of math—fractal mathematics—is dedicated to developing ways of dealing with a world that won't conform to the human brain's make-it-nice-and-neat desires for a tidy architecture. And that is the reason the mysterious powers behind reality put Water Hands on Earth: to remind their order-obsessed Air Hand companions that the world (and certainly their beautiful, artistic, and oh-so-elegant Water Hand companions) will never be as organized as they'd like it to be.

And it's still okay.

# A Brief Look at the Oil and Water Combinations

Some hand types do not naturally go together. In the old-school books on palmistry, these opposites are usually warned to steer clear of each other; but as we've said, we have learned that the world is just not that simple.

In the modern world of relationships, opposites *do* attract and find ways to accommodate (and relish!) their differences. So in this section we won't be talking about whether couples with radically different hand types can make a go of it but how they go about working out the differences to create something deep and lasting.

## WATER AND FIRE

In classical palmistry water and fire look as if they had nothing to offer one another. Indeed, they seem antagonistic. The Water Hand type is very much into details, into taking her sweet time. Fire is not into details and wants to pick up the tempo—now, not later. If this looks like a crisis in the making, with two dance partners stepping out, not only to different tunes but also different dances—well, we have to say in our most authority-filled voice that it simply doesn't work that way.

Yes, the relationships between Water Hand and

Fire Hand will be interesting to say the least. But it's doable. Not only is it doable, but many couples turn it into an absolute art form, achieving an astounding depth and togetherness.

In the relationship of Water Hand to Fire Hand, we see an appreciation of the qualities that the hand types share. For Water and Fire, it's the ability to flow that they both share. In couples like this we usually find they have a tendency to change jobs easily in their careers; and far from generating crisis, this makes for excitement and added closeness in the relationship. What is happening here is that the love of change that's part of the Fire Hand's worldview is answered by the love of flow and adaptability of the Water Hand.

In these relationships, we've noticed that the Water Hand has to be truly aware of not smothering the Fire Hand. However, mastering this trick is one that the Water Hand—one of the more adaptable of all the Hand Types—is up for.

Of course, avoiding smothering your significant other and allowing her breathing space is something we *all* have to do, no matter what our hand type.

## ADVICE FOR THE WATER HAND
## (ABOUT YOUR FIERY PARTNER)

How much drama do you like in your life? Your Fire Hand will definitely be all about increasing the theatrical in the life you lead together. Flash, dazzle, an all-singing, all-dancing, at-all-times-and-all-places approach to the world—that's what you should expect when you spend quality time with your significant and fiery other. You'll become intimately acquainted with her creative ways of adding sparkle and movement to even the smallest of life's moments. An invitation to the most mundane social event, like a birthday or a dinner party, can develop into something more closely resembling outtakes from *Indiana Jones and the Temple of Doom*. Of course, as a Water Hand, you're naturally (even shall we say, *extremely*?) adaptable, more adaptable than your partner by orders of magnitude, with an uncanny skill for handling the up and downs, ins and outs of life with style, wit, and grace. This skill will be much needed (and should provide some comfort) when your Fire Hand partner makes you a part of the highly dramatic situations that arrive at your shared doorstep as regularly as clockwork.

Of course, your adaptability and tranquility under fire will rub off on your Fire Hand. Eventually, this will be a very significant part of her attraction to you—the fact that you *don't* panic (as quickly as she does) and don't tend to go ballistic at every setback or any time you both experience the all too common slings and arrows of outrageous fortune. Because, as a Fire Hand, she hardly ever feels emotions in small increments and tends to super-size everything, never giving back to the world a nudge when a good old-fashioned shove will do, your coolness under fire will help her react to the world in gentler, kinder, and, many times, more effective, ways.

### ADVICE FOR THE FIRE HAND (ABOUT YOUR WATERY PARTNER)

They're so adaptable, these Water Hands—at times (can we admit it?) *maddeningly* adaptable. He seems to be able to make room for any and every possible change in circumstance without as much as a peep. Doesn't he understand that the world needs to be responded to *right now* in big red letters—with a megaphone? Time to man the barricades, to just say NO!

The phrase "go with the flow" was invented to describe your partner's behavior, and at times this willingness to go along and get along can cause your blood pressure to rise more than a bit.

Take a deep breath.

Actually, it's best to appreciate that in any partnership your significant other can give you access to qualities, talents, and strategies you might lack. Let's face it, as a Fire Hand, patience is not your long suit. Stirring up the world, advocating right-now right-here change—yes, that's your talent. Not infrequently you might think about employing just a bit more diplomacy in your dealings with the rest of the world. True?

Enter the Water Hand.

Although his patience and coolness can sometimes be puzzling when you're impatient to get things done, you'll profit (need we say, greatly?) if you can just slow down for a moment and realize that he just might have a point. If you do slow down, if you do use just a bit more diplomacy in your attempts to change the world, you might be able to arrive at your destination just a little bit faster, thanks to the aid of his Water Hand talents.

And—Fire Hand—isn't faster *always* better?

# Air and Earth

The earth abides, while air goes where it will.
This is another one of those relationships that the
old books warn is doomed to come in last and
limping. The logic here is that the restlessness and
love of the intellect and detail that is a part of the
Air Hand personality will not jibe with an Earth
Hand's active do-it-yourself and do-it-now phi-
losophy of life. But in the successful Earth
Hand–Air Hand relationships we've seen, there is
a smooth flow between the talents of the different
hand styles. Earth does not smother air; air does
not flee from the solid, productive capabilities of
earth. Most often what occurs is that the projects
the Earth Hand undertakes are supported and organized by the superior organizational skills of
the Air Hand. Air Hands are usually masters of
communication—and there is no project on the
face of the planet that can't benefit from a talented spokesperson for it. What happens in
these productive Earth Hand–Air Hand relationships is a productive partnership, each partner
yielding to the other's expertise. We've noticed
that couples with this capability are scrupulous

about giving one another credit for their triumphs in the area of their expertise. It's one of the features that seem to give the relationship stability and longevity.

The Air Hand's ability to create excitement about the Earth Hand's projects lends a sparkle to the efforts he could gain in no other way. The Earth Hand can help organize the Air Hand's projects into real-world practicalities that go from being dreams to actual realities in the world of nine to five.

One of the things we've noticed is that in Air Hand–Earth Hand relationships, there are times of withdrawal into the home-as-castle fortress. In this case, both hand styles jealously guard the home as a place of togetherness and a place to recharge the batteries. When you call the Air Hand–Earth Hand couple, do not expect to have someone pick up the phone on the first ring. You'll be disappointed. These couples pick up only for true intimates, insiders—those people who (although they may not be related by actual DNA) are part of the couple's twenty-first-century virtual family.

## ADVICE TO THE EARTH HAND
## (ABOUT YOUR AIRY PARTNER)

Here's some good advice for Earth Hands pursuing a relationship with an Air Hand companion. Some people are afraid of walking under ladders or of opening umbrellas indoors, but for Air Hands, the fear is of losing the commodity that's most precious of all to them: their freedom.

Want to push the buttons of an Air Hand? Begin teasing him about his fear of getting trapped, losing his mobility, his ability (and hope) of a future that includes going anywhere, doing anything. While you, as an Earth Hand, look forward to stability, a future of comfortable, repeated experiences, this is not the case with your Air Hand. The vision of peace and stability that seems so promising to you will seem like a jail sentence—a trip to a dreary Devil's Island of sameness and stagnation.

Is the glass half-full or half-empty? For an Air Hand looking at an endless future of more of the same thing, a repetition of identical, unchanging days—the glass is not only half-empty but also not worth sipping. He will look at it as a sign that the time is ripe for escape—always a favorite activity in the life of Air Hands.

This does not mean that in an Earth Hand–Air Hand relationship, the Air Hand will be allergic to a stable, warm family life. In fact he prefers home situations in which the my-home-is-my-castle effect is the law. The Air Hand, with his love of rushing around, has a deep desire for the kind of relaxation that allows him to take a rest from his abundant nervous energy. After a day of frantic up-and-down, he quickly becomes addicted to the downtime represented by family, by home.

One of the lessons that you, as an Earth Hand having a relationship with an Air Hand, must learn (the sooner, the better) is to deemphasize that part of the relationship that speaks of long-term committedness, and just let it happen. Although you love to feel yourself walking on and planning for a solid foundation, in this case you just have to be patient. After all, Earth abides, doesn't it?

If you're considering a relationship with an Air Hand, you should be aware that from time to time you'll find yourself wondering if your companion *ever* takes life seriously. After all (will be your Earth Hand style thinking) if you want to accomplish anything during this particular lifetime, you'll have to buckle down and *do* something—not just think about it. Allow us to give you just a bit of *Palms Up!* advice before you get started, Earth Hand. In dealing with a significant other who happens to be an Air Hand, the straight-on, just-the-facts-ma'am confrontation style is *not* going to get you to the destination you desire. Highly improbable.

What will get your always-flying-this-way-and-that Air Hand partner to take seriously the matters that *you* think are most important? An indirect approach works wonders in communications between Earth Hands and Air Hands. Instead of complaining about the flighty, here-there-and-everywhere approach, the favorite style of the Air Hand, try using the following simple phrase: "You know one thing you're not considering here . . ." At the end of this sentence, tack on the matter that's on your mind. It sounds simple, but often it works, because Air Hands are always restlessly looking for something new, something novel, something that, indeed, they've never considered.

Air Hands are always seeking newness. And what's more, they're delighted when they find it. As an Earth Hand, there will be many things you think about and ponder as you focus on your next project, because building and creating are of great concern to you—and your projects are like catnip to the always curious Air Hand. This can work wonders when trying to get your Air Hand other to focus on doing things.

And don't assume that your mindscape is at all familiar to your Air Hand partner. It won't be. In fact the way you view the world, how you believe people should act in it, your priorities, and the way you personally organize them will appear as a completely alien world to him, a fascinating alien world.

From gaining his interest in a subject to actually involving him in a project is a short step, easily negotiated. The only caveat: If you want an Air Hand to stop flitting about and focus on accomplishing something in the real world, *don't present it in a my-way-or-the-highway* manner. As an

Earth Hand, you focus on an activity to complete it. The Air Hand will focus on an activity only to learn how to do it. The Earth Hand approach is practical. The Air Hand approach is intellectual. An Earth Hand is proud when he can point to a thing and say, "I did that!" An Air Hand will be proud to say, "I know how to do that!"

The difference may seem subtle, but it means everything in the way that Earth Hands and Air Hands relate to one another.

## ADVICE FOR THE AIR HAND (ABOUT YOUR EARTHY PARTNER)

Although at times your Earth Hand partner will seem to be overly practical, insisting that simply *everything* must have its own point and purpose, it's one of those characteristics you'll learn to live with, even benefit from. Can we admit that at times as an Air Hand you tend to love information and details just for their own sake? And can you also confess that you do tend to just think about many more projects than you'll ever actually try to turn into a reality? Yes, making things happen in the real world is definitely something you might learn from the Earth Hand way of dealing with the world. You'll grow as an individual if you occasionally try to take the information you've amassed and attempt to actually *do* something with it in the real world.

Something practical?

Yes, that *would* be the Earth hand partner's approach to the problem.

So although at times you may be annoyed with the completely alien way in which your Earth Hand partner seems to think everything in the world should turn into something tangible and usable, you should also see how hitchhiking on some of his way of thinking might be good for you. You might even learn something. And as an Air Hand the act of learning, of amassing even *more* information, has a definite appeal. After all, as an Air Hand, learning is your thing.

## Earth and Fire

The last time you thought about earth and fire together, you were probably watching a special on The Learning Channel. You watched the earth open up and spew red hot lava that flowed across the ground in smoking rivers. This is the classic warning old-school palmistry books deliver: fire burns earth. And although we will admit that the combination does indeed generate much heat, the reality is (as always) much more complicated than the old books make out.

After all, there are those who prefer to burn. Earth Hand and Fire Hand couples tend to be people who are interested in making their mark, usually full of ambition, locked together in their excitement about something, whether it's career, family, or saving the world. The Earth Hand–Fire Hand combination is one that appeals to couples who would actually begin to chafe if a relationship got too comfortable. These couples love and crave high drama; their relationships seem to be always on the verge of becoming an epic movie, or opera, where life isn't worth living if it isn't lived large. In thinking about the Earth Hand–Fire Hand relationship, it's best to remember the romantic poets like Byron and Shelley, whose lives were intense, even shocking. They burned.

And so do some modern-day folks. Although they hold down responsible jobs like everyone else, standing in line at Starbucks waiting for their double-latte to get them started in the work-a-day morning, they have secret identities that come out when the working day is done. After they've punched the time clock and done their daily best to pay the rent, they come out of the phone booth like Clark Kent in the old Superman movies and assume another, more radical identity. Modern romantics.

There's always something a bit extreme about these individuals. Their clothing tends to be extreme. They have a taste for exotic food. There's always a Harley in the garage, no matter how young or old they are.

With that said, you can see that the Earth Hand–Fire Hand combination is not for everyone, and it is also fair to say that not every couple that attempts this combination is able to bring it off successfully. The unsuccessful attempt to merge the fiery and willful ways of the Fire Hand with the real-world sensibilities of the Earth Hand can result in more high drama than either partner wishes for in their life. These unsuccessful Earth Hand–Fire Hand relationships can result in long-held grudges and wounds that take a long time to heal.

Still, when such a combination is successful, it is truly something to behold: romance on a grand scale. It's the kind of romantic duo perpetually celebrated on the screens of neighborhood multiplexes and theatrical stages, going all the way back to Shakespeare and before. It smolders; it burns. But, after all, isn't love what makes the world go round?

## ADVICE FOR THE EARTH HAND (ABOUT YOUR FIERY PARTNER)

Although as an Earth Hand, your life is caught up in practicalities—how to make things happen right here, right now—in the real world, you've become attracted to the flashy ways of a Fire Hand partner. The relationship you've signed on for will almost doubtlessly be tempestuous enough at times to make *The Young and the Restless* look pale and un-dramatic in comparison.

Our advice?

Expect the unexpected. The Fire Hand will definitely be advocating for more life changes at a faster rate than you will usually feel comfortable with, but you'll never be bored or complacent about the relationship. Expect misunderstandings.

Remember, as two very different kinds of people, the early years will be the most challenging. Until you learn to adapt to your Fire Hand partner's flair for drama and change, you may feel like you're attempting to master an extreme sport like out-of-bounds skiing. Earth Hand/Fire Hand relationships tend to be highly volatile in the early stages and then settle down. Be patient and open-minded. Big rewards come to those who wait. Remember: Earth abides.

## ADVICE FOR THE FIRE HAND (ABOUT YOUR EARTHY PARTNER)

In the early stages of an Earth Hand–Fire Hand relationship, you're bound to feel at least some frustration with the slower pace of your partner. You're impetuous; he's thoughtful, steady. Although his ability to make dramatic things happen in the real world and his participation in often stunning, high-profile projects can be tremendously exciting in a way that enhances your sense of life's drama, you may at times feel that events are moving at an annoyingly glacial pace.

Since, as a Fire Hand, you have a talent for inspiring other people, use it. One of the things that's drawn your Earth Hand partner to you is your ability to make him see beyond the here and now, to glimpse possibilities that few others see. When you find yourself in a funk about the fact that life seems to have settled down to the kind of same-thing-everyday state you are deeply allergic to, use your knack for inspiring others to inspire your Earth Hand partner to the Next Big Thing. Your ability to make important changes in your most intimate relationship will help you see beyond present dissatisfactions to a future full of promise. Remember, if they can maintain their equilibrium, Earth Hand–Fire Hand relationships grow sweeter and spicier with age; they retain their vitality when other less volatile combinations have lost their spark. For this reason they're well worth the sometimes intense effort needed to maintain them in the early stages.

# Taking It Farther

Of course, once you've paired up partners and explored their hand shape possibilities, you've only just started your work as a palm reader. By now, you've learned a lot about the art of palm reading as it's practiced in the here and now of the twenty-first century. You've learned how to look at the thumb, tell whether the length of the fingers qualify someone as a big picture type or a detail-oriented Sherlock. You also know how to create a lot of fun by exploring if any of the couples you've chosen has a True Seer or a La Mancha as a member.

Sit back, now, and relax as we show you a few examples of taking the Hand Game and your skills as a *Palms Up!* palm reader to the next level.

# Who Is the Most Stubborn?

Once you've had the various duos look at their different hand shapes, you're ready to take a look at their thumbs—and get a few laughs in the process (something that no party should have in short supply). Whatever hand pairing (fire with water, earth with air) you've been working with, ask them if they're curious about who, between the two of them, is the most stubborn. Look for the person in the couple with the longest, most prominent top phalange on the thumb. And don't assume it will be the male. Then begin comparing the thumbs of the various couples in the room. Go on to look for Lookers and Leapers and point them out. Remember, if the thumb's top phalange is bigger than the lower phalange, you're looking at a Leaper: This person tends to make decisions quickly, leaping into choices and going with whatever her intuition or gut instinct tells her. If the person's a Looker, the lower phalange will be longer than the top phalange. This is someone who will never make a decision before she's done the math and run all the spreadsheets. And she never pays sticker price for anything!

## Who's into Details?

Once you've taken a close look at each pair of thumbs, it's time to proceed to taking stock of the length of fingers for each couple.

This time around, you'll let them discover whether their partner is (or is not) into details. First describe the qualities of the fingers. Remember, if the person has long fingers, details are his thing. If the person has short fingers, he's a big picture sort. For the long-fingered hand types like water and air, you'll point out that here are the Sherlocks of this world, seeing and observing everything they come across in their daily lives. For the fire and earth types with their short fingers, you'll describe the world as they like to see it, from a forest-not-the-trees viewpoint that helps them make sense of the fast-changing world around them. For example, if you come across a long-fingered Water Hand coupled with a short-fingered Fire Hand, you can tease them about the differences in their pictures of the world. "She's into details," you might say to the Water Hand. "But not necessarily organized." Take hold of her Fire Hand companion's short-fingered hand. "He's *not* into details so much. She's the Sherlock. He's the Sky Pilot."

People will be amazed at your insightfulness.

As you become more comfortable and confident with your abilities as a palm reader, you'll be able to tell each couple more about themselves and their possibilities as couples—both romantic and otherwise. You might consider looking at their Life Lines and telling them who's the Hot

Chile Pepper and who is more the Jazz on the Veranda type.

Always end your palm reading with something that takes in the group as whole. One way to do this is to walk through a group and look at their Head Lines. Then reveal who among them always makes her appointments (next Wednesday at 3:35 in the plaza!) and arrives on time (the True Seers) and who in the group is always late (the La Manchas, who are too caught up in the thump and rattle of the world to remember just when and where he was planning to get together with his True Seer friends).

Using your knowledge of the palm is a sure path to popularity. Even better, your skills will get people talking, breaking out of their party ruts. And, who can tell? In bringing other people closer together, you may even stumble across that someone just right for you, that person who might turn out to be just your particular cup of tea.

We've seen it happen more than once.

# Squares, Triangles, Stars, and Other Markings

There are literally hundreds of markings on the palm that have significance.

Since the purpose of our guide is to teach you how to have fun with palmistry (and to avoid driving the people whose hands you'll be reading into a state resembling coma), we're going to touch on just the highlights—what we consider the Big Four.

# What Are the Big Four?

Probably the most important of the palm formations to know are squares, triangles, crosses, and stars. These lines or markings are sometimes found adrift on the palm, sometimes on the major lines like the Life Line, the Head Line, and the Heart Line. Each of these marks has a story to tell. You can have a lot of fun telling your friends and significant others the stories these marks whisper to you . . .

When starting out, we recommend that you begin by looking for these markings on the person's dominant hand.

# Squares

The square is like a stout wall enclosing an area it wishes to protect. In such an area, you'll find a feature that's missing in much of modern life—sanctuary. One of the neat features of the square is that often you can tell just exactly *when* it occurred in a person's life, because the square (nine times out of ten) will be something the person actually *felt*—a time when there was a noticeable (and sometimes remarkable) sense of peace that came into their life.

## What Does a Square Look Like?

Well, of course, the square looks like a square. Roughly. When trying to locate a square on a person's palm, you're looking for a collection of lines that make up a squareish sort of structure. The organic, loosely drawn quality of the square is also true of all the various markings we are going to look at here: triangles, crosses, and stars.

## Where Is the Square?

Where the square is located can tell you where the person will have protection, in what areas of his life.

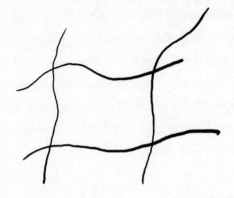

## The Square

AT THE BASE OF THE THUMB

We're humans. We make mistakes. But if you have a square located at the very base of the thumb, you'll find that, for the most part, you'll be able to avoid the worst effects of your most misguided decisions. Plus, you're likely to make fewer mistakes than others. (We don't recommend tempting fate, however.)

## AT THE BASE OF THE
## INDEX FINGER

This is traditionally known as the teacher's square. What the square in this area reveals is that you have an almost instinctive sense of comfort in your public life. People with this mark are extremely comfortable with getting up in front of other people and explaining things; they feel safe expressing themselves in public. The teacher's square is especially beneficial for people who make their living doing training, a skill that's more and more necessary, and more and more prized in the world we live in. People who possess the teacher's square are often easygoing in situations where most feel like they have something (either consciously or unconsciously) to prove. Not if you have the teacher's square.

## AT THE BASE OF THE
## MIDDLE FINGER

If you have a square at the base of your middle finger, you are likely to be the kind of person who will find support, even protection, from the world around you, especially from members of your own community, your friends, your family.

Everyone gets into trouble at times. If you find this happy symbol at the base of your middle finger, you can look to others for help. We recommend that you prime the pump (so to speak) and remember to help others in their hour of need. The *Palms Up!* reader always remembers that what goes around, comes around.

AT THE BASE OF THE RING FINGER
If you find a square at the base of your ring finger, you're a supporter of the arts, a person who looks on creativity much as some people look at religion—a person who will draw actual sustenance from art, and the idea of art in hard times. People who have this configuration tend to see art—and, in many ways, civilization—as the highest possible flowering of humanity, the thing that keeps us moving forward toward something worthy and worth preserving. They are drawn to both artists and art in a deeply respectful way.

Many times people with this configuration are drawn to each other; the feeling (and attraction) seems to be mutual. We have noticed that frequently people with this mark choose those who have deep creative streaks as significant others and romantic objects. Sometimes these people will be artists (with a capital *A*), and sometimes they will be people who in parts of their life—some very unusual—display a deep streak of creativity.

### AT THE BASE OF THE BABY FINGER

Mercury is a bandit. We mean that in the very nicest way possible. Those who have an emphasis on the baby finger—the one finger of the hand that is associated with Mercury and communication—have just a little bit of the outlaw in their makeup. It is not that they're necessarily rebellious in any way. No, it's that they're just the smallest bit . . . slippery. They tend to be somewhat silver tongued, and they're capable, as we've pointed out elsewhere in this book, of stretching the truth from time to time. Their friends and loved ones are comfortable if not exactly fully accepting of Mercury's sketchy way with the facts, and (we hope) they find it charming. Or so bandit Mercury likes to think.

Because those in whom Mercury is emphasized are not completely immune to their own blandishments, they tell stories that are just a wee bit exaggerated. Later they forget that they have significantly stretched the facts of the story and accept them as completely truthful (and unmodified) versions of what really happened.

If you find a square under your baby finger, you'll probably still tell those tall tales, but you'll be protected from their worst effects. You will be considered colorful rather than an out-and-out liar, endearing rather than scamming. We've also noticed that those with this mark on their hands can talk you out of your own eye-teeth!

# Triangles

Triangles give energy. To remember this, we like to picture the alleged power given by the pyramids. The triangle is the most stable of all physical objects, and when you find these smart little shapes on the palm of a person you're reading for, you'll be able to give her good news. The triangle is one mark that adds energy and flexibility wherever it's found.

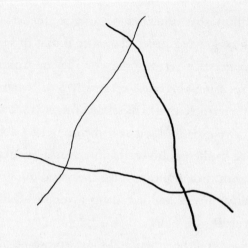

**The Triangle**

# On the Mounts: Adding Energy

When you find a triangle at the base of one of the fingers, it will add energy, flexibility, and suppleness to the power that the finger is all about. Triangles represent energy and, to some extent, flexibility and grace. Think of a classically trained dancer, someone who has spent enough time training her body that it moves with suppleness and flow that others aren't able to muster. This kind of gracefulness can also be found in people who practice serious yoga or Pilates. Although we're using this idea as a metaphor, when we find a triangle under the index finger (for example), we'll be looking at someone who's able to move in the public world (the world of finance, the world of politics) with the same unnerving facility that a trained dancer might. Get the picture?

Let's roll the video, and show you some of the ways that this (sort of) pyramid power works.

## AT THE BASE OF THE THUMB

If you have a triangle conspicuously located under the base of the thumb, you are adept at making decisions. Whether you're a Leaper or a Looker, you will, as you mature, become more and more facile with the art of decision making. This usually means possessing a sense of when to say "Go!" and when to say "No!" that to lesser mortals looks nothing less than uncanny.

## AT THE BASE OF THE
## INDEX FINGER

X does not mark the spot, but the triangle does; and when it's at the base of the index finger, you'll find both the dealers and the wheelers, people comfortable with the give and take of negotiation. Usually this facility with negotiation means that, if you possess a triangle at the base of your index finger, you will have a comfort level with the financial that few others possess, and you may even acquire other people who depend on you for financial advice. A triangle under the index finger indicates that you're comfortable in public life and the art of the deal.

## AT THE BASE OF THE
## MIDDLE FINGER

A triangle at the base of the middle finger can be the mark of major schmoozer, the person who lives to make connections with the people in their community. This mark usually indicates deep ties with family and friends, but it can also be a sign that the person so endowed has the skills (and drive) to be an important mover and shaker with community charity work and organizations. We sometimes see this mark on people active in the local chamber of commerce. If you have a triangle located at the base of the middle finger, you're likely to be a person who will be able to make friends easily and quickly, regardless of the barriers.

Barriers? Some people can feel just fine making conversations with friends when they come to them on familiar ground, places where they feel safe—at home or work. But if individuals come in contact with new people in unfamiliar places, like a party at a stranger's house or the house of a friend of a friend, they find themselves unable to deploy the sparkling and relaxed conversation that they are used to in places of comfort and zones of safety.

Not so for you with the triangle under your middle finger. Everyone is a part of your community, or quickly becomes so. You are the kind of person who, if you find yourself sharing space in an igloo with a number of Eskimos, will—even without knowledge of the language (Inuit? Yupik?)—make friends. A quality like this is apt to make you very successful and well liked. Want to locate a true schmoozer? Check out the base of the middle finger for a triangle.

### AT THE BASE OF THE RING FINGER

Got a triangle at the base of the ring finger? You have a sense of aesthetics. Sometimes it's in the way you move—a certain grace, a certain elegance. You possess character. You have taste with a capital *T*. Your friends ask you, "Does this color look good on me?" and they actually listen and—even more amazing—take your advice.

The triangle gives you an aesthetic sense that keeps you looking cool—even when you're not. And when you have to go from one radically different kind of event to another and don't have time to change, the people at the second party don't think you haven't dressed appropriately, they wonder if this is the new thing, the latest fashion. Because a casual elegance seems to come so easily to you, you're easy to hate. But any umbrage others take won't last long. It's *way* too easy to forgive those who bring a sense of beauty and style into the world. Let's face it, you can get away with murder.

You've got to think outside the box about this one. Sometimes conventional beauty is not the way a triangle under the ring finger shows itself. At times these lucky earthlings manifest the trait of terminal cuteness, the ability to get the attention of all and sundry simply by being themselves. You can stand right next to such a person and set yourself on fire—to absolutely no avail. A triangle at the base of the ring finger is in the house, and all eyes naturally flow to him.

## AT THE BASE OF THE BABY FINGER

As a *Palms Up!* palm reader you know by now that the baby finger is all about communication. A triangle at the base of the baby finger will reveal a gift of gab energizing the mercurial tendencies of the littlest (but not least) of the finger family. In thinking about the triangle here, you will find that the possessors of this mark view communication in a way (and with a fondness) that few others do. If you have a triangle at the base of your baby finger, you have deep skills in the area of verbal communication and a need to use them, frequently.

The other people in your sphere of interest will both be charmed and driven a little bonkers by this aspect of your personality. The fact is you are fascinated by the act of communication and by great talkers. The triangle at the base of the baby finger is a little like a verbal writer's fork. As you recall, the writer's fork (a fork at the end of the Head Line) indicates that its possessor has deep resources whenever they want to communicate in writing. We frequently find people with this mark have a tendency to make some part of their living in the world of written communication. Here you find editors, writers, people who work in advertising and television.

A triangle at the base of the baby finger indicates that the bearer of this mark has skills aplenty in the area of talk. If you've got this mark, think about a career as a talk-show personality, a DJ, a corporate spokesperson. You might find yourself excelling at professions where talk is of the essence.

# The Cross

In old-style palmistry, the cross is looked on with suspicion as a sign of possible danger and lack of luck. But for the *Palms Up!* reader, this mark is less fraught with peril and danger.

The cross represents a crossroads—a moment when the universe is on the move in a person's life, a moment when a decision will be called for, even perhaps a moment of high drama (no one passes through life without drama aplenty). But unlike the old-school palm reader's take on this mark, we believe that it does not indicate an unhappy outcome.

This point, although seemingly small, is not without substance.

Choice and change are inevitable. And depending on the choices we make, our lives change—sometimes for better, sometimes for worse. To the *Palms Up!* reader, this is what the cross on the palm represents: crossroads, change points. Crosses do not, we repeat, do not signify ill luck when found on the palm. Crosses represent the arrival of a bridge that you'll jump across when you come to it. Decisions to make. Just as

with the other marks on the palm, where they occur can tell you a lot about where in life these big
change points will occur.

## On the Life Line

If you have a cross on the Life Line, you can use
its position on this important line to tell you
when a decision point, a crossroads will be
reached. Like a terrible tease, this cross will tell
you when, but it will give you absolutely no information about the area of life affected by this
bridge to be crossed.

### HOW DO I READ TIME ON
### THE LIFE LINE?

If you find a cross on your Life Line and want to
determine just when this decision point might
have happened or will be happening, remember
the following:

• The Life Line's beginning place is between the index finger and the thumb. The
place where it starts represents your birth
and early life.

• The Life Line's middle represents about age thirty-five, midlife, time to think about health insurance and IRAs.
• The Life Line ends at the bottom of the hand. This area represents the time—your late eighties, early nineties—when you'll want to think about taking your first longevity treatments to begin your second life as a post-teenager. Ah, the wonders of twenty-first-century science!

From this timeline, you should be able to tell when the decision point represented by the cross should occur. Of course, the only way you'll be able to tell what this decision point is about is to make a *Palms Up!* reader educated guess.

What do we mean by this? Here are some *Palms Up!* reader educated guesses:

• A cross in the early twenties? This might indicate a decision about the choice of a romantic partner. If you're reading the palm of someone in her early twenties, ask her if she's thinking of moving in with someone.

• A cross in the early thirties? Career time is happening now. You might think about asking if she's thinking about a career change in the near future.

• A cross in the early forties? Is the person wondering if her main relationship is working out for her? Is she wondering whether to put everything into keeping this relationship alive or to admit that it's just not working out and it's time to move on?

• A cross in the early fifties? Surprisingly, more and more people are beginning to look at early retirement and considering second careers. Ask if she's thinking about what to do with the second part of her life.

## A Cross on the Mounts

Since crosses are about decision points in a person's life, you can look for crosses at the base of each of the fingers to give you information about the areas in which you will face a crossroads, a place where life will challenge you to give a yes-or-no decision.

## AT THE BASE OF THE THUMB

If you have a cross at the base of your thumb, you have a major decision to make about who or what to make a commitment to. This usually indicates a need to take steps to overhaul the very way you make decisions and to be very, very careful to make sure that your decisions are making you happy, not just satisfying the needs of those around you. This mark often indicates the judicious use of a bit of creative selfishness.

## AT THE BASE OF THE
## INDEX FINGER

A cross at the base of the index finger is one of the most obvious (and more frequent) places to find a cross. If you have one, the cross indicates that an important business decision needs to be made. Quite often you also find that this is an indication of an important career change in the offing. Changing from one career to another? Changing companies but doing the same thing? Making a decision about more traveling in your current job? All of these can be indicated by a cross at the base of the index finger.

## AT THE BASE OF THE
## MIDDLE FINGER

A cross at the base of your middle finger indicates you'll have a crossroads-style decision to make about your relationship to the community of which you are a part. This can indicate major decisions about family or friends, but it can also indicate more public and sometimes political decisions. When you find a cross beneath the middle finger, it's all about choice, all about the time for decisions. The cross means that the choice will be yours to make.

## AT THE BASE OF THE
## RING FINGER

A cross at the base of the ring finger gives you taste in the aesthetic side of life that is well formed and (usually) deeply opinionated. This is frequently found in people involved in the arts—film, dance, literature, or painting—who are in the role of directing or producing. For you, decision making will be natural and instinctive, rising out of a kind of knack. You will know what is right—and what is wrong—about an aesthetic production, and your judgments will rise out of a deep aesthetic sense that is as natural as the grain in a beautiful piece of wood. Life will always be interesting (even, at times, contentious) for people who possess this mark. Everyone thinks you're an expert when it comes to creativity (after all, you know what you like!). However, in a professional capacity, it takes someone with objectivity and truthfulness to assess a work of art and how an audience will perceive it. Not everyone has the objectivity to do this tough task.

### AT BASE OF THE BABY FINGER

Remember, the baby finger is all about communication, and when you find a cross at the base of your baby finger, you're a person who will be faced with issues and choices about whether to hold fast to information or to spread it around. Frequently, this mark is fairly binary, indicating a person who is utterly trustworthy with his communication—able to take the secrets to the grave—or someone who loves to gossip, knows every secret (who's sleeping with whom, who just broke up with whom, and who's going in for a tummy tuck at the end of the month) and usually has a phone tree to spread the word around. Again, the cross in this instance reveals that you will have many decisions to make about the information that is yours.

## The Mystic Cross

Many people have heard about the Mystic Cross, and we are always asked about it. Although the Mystic Cross is a rare line, you do very occasionally run across it, winking up at you from a palm or two. Because it's one of the celebrities in the palm-reading world, we should probably let you know about it, just in case you run into it sometime when it's wearing a pair of Fendi sunglasses and a Shibori hand-dyed silk scarf.

There are crosses, and then there are crosses. The Mystic Cross is one of those *other* ones. You'll find this cross in the area between the Heart Line and the Head Line. It won't be just *any* cross. Like any true celebrity, the Mystic Cross stands alone, all by itself. It does not touch either the Head or Heart Lines, and it is not touched by any other smaller lines. It is, so to speak, free and clear. If you keep this fact in mind, you'll be able to call your shots accurately.

So, what is the Mystic Cross all about? If you find the Mystic Cross on someone's hand, it's a safe bet that she has a fairly robust sense of intuition, probably from a very early age. These are the kind of people who usually display an uncanny ability to know who's going to be calling before they pick up the phone. Although they aren't always able to use this knack for uncanny guessing to their advantage, they usually have times when they're just simply on, very much like a gambler on a lucky streak.

Probably the most interesting configuration is when the Mystic Cross is found marked clearly on the hands of a couple in a relationship. This seems to work both to their advantage and great disadvantage. Imagine: You're in touch with your significant other and able to (almost) reliably tune in to what your partner is thinking, feeling, her moods both good and bad. A couple like this not only can make each other feel more wonderful than anyone else in the world but can also inspire long journeys through the dark side of personal relationships.

But generally it's a good thing. Those blessed with the Mystic Cross are usually able to help themselves and others with their gut instincts, and the Mystic Cross acts like a spark in their lives. People with the skills of the Mystic Cross are able to give hope to people when they feel there is no hope and serve to hint to us that there is more to life than simply earning a living, growing gradually older, and looking for a way to erase the lines we've earned on our face from a lifetime of smiling and frowning. It is as if they were a gift from some other world where people can, quite effortlessly, see a bigger, more inclusive picture.

# A Few Last Words

Now that you've made it to the end of this book, you'll be able look into the palms of friends and strangers alike and stun them with your insights into their lives.

But this is only the beginning of the *Palms Up!* journey. Once you've mastered the techniques in *Palms Up!*, you'll probably want to explore further. We do not pretend that this book does more than scratch the surface of the material available on palmistry.

Where do you go to learn more about palm reading? Books can take you a fair distance. The availability of works on the art of palmistry has never been more widespread. At Amazon's web site, typing the words *palm reading* into the search engine brings up more than ninety thousand hits to explore. Although you won't need to read even a small fraction of those books to have fun with palm reading, there are a few books that will broaden your horizons as a twenty-first-century palmist, and two authors we recommend.

Around the turn of the last century, William Benham was one of the first individuals to make a focused attempt to turn palm reading into a truly analytical art. Like wildlife painter John James Audubon, who made thousands of drawings of birds, Benham collected photographs of hands to examine and was tireless in his pursuit of knowledge of the mysteries of the hand. In *The Laws of Scientific Hand Reading,* Benham lays out his theories of palmistry. For anyone wishing to gaze deeply into the art of hand reading, his writings are wonderful resources. While not the easiest read, they're fascinating looks at an early attempt to analyze palm reading.

We would also like to recommend Richard Webster. Webster is one of the modern masters of palmistry. He hails from Auckland, New

Zealand, and has written about and advanced the subject of palmistry more than anyone else alive today. This soft-spoken New Zealander with a twinkle in his eye is one of the most personable and well-versed thinkers on the topic of palm reading. Webster is thoroughly well-traveled and has used his travels, particularly in India, to master the cross-cultural aspects of palmistry. He's explored the art of Indian thumb reading—a fascination of Indian palm readers, who (as we've mentioned) will spend entire sessions solely on the lines of the thumb. An acknowledged feng shui master, Webster has inspired and taught more people to read palms through his books and talks than any other twenty-first-century master of palmistry.

As a *Palms Up!* palm reader, you'll spend most of your time interacting with old friends and new acquaintances in a friendly, upbeat way. Remember to tread lightly as you give your readings; be gentle and approach everyone whose palm you read with an open and honest respect. Never forget that the real purpose of palm reading is entertainment, to give people a glimpse of themselves that will bring a thrilled smile to their faces.

Never take yourself—or the palms you read—too seriously. It will get in the way of real insights.

Like us, we hope you'll come to feel a deep gratitude toward the people who let you enter their world. This gratitude comes from being able to trace through the lines on a complete stranger's palm the human elements and issues that connect us to people in distant places, living in circumstances that differ markedly from our own. As you practice your *Palms Up!* palm reading, you'll come to see the human hand as a kind of map that will lead you to be more deeply aware of the world you live in—and the mysteries of your own self.